The Connection Between Money and Seed Sowing

How to Grow Your Money and Achieve Financial Freedom

Eric Tangumonkem, Ph.D.

IEM PRESS

PO Box 831001, Richardson, TX 75080

A Subsidiary of IEM APPROACH

ISBN 13: 978-1-63603-127-9
Library of Congress Catalog Card Number: 2021952223

Dedication

To all those who have fallen prey to the gimmicks of unscrupulous financial preachers and voracious wolves in sheep's clothing.

To all who sincerely want to learn how to prosper holistically. It is possible to be a believer in the Lord Jesus Christ and prosper simultaneously.

Table of Contents

Introduction

About a decade ago, I had a conversation that troubled me greatly. This conversation was centered around poverty in Africa, corruption, disease, lack of infrastructure, etc. The person I was talking with said that those in America have their heaven on earth, but those in Africa will have their share when they go to heaven. This person seriously believed that the wealth and affluence in the West was somehow an indication of spiritual apathy; meanwhile, the poverty and lack in Africa was a mark of spiritual superiority.

There are those who believe that poverty is a sign of spirituality and pious living. Those who hold to such a belief point to the type of life Jesus Christ lived, highlighting that He did not have material possessions and that the early disciples suffered martyrdom and were poor. According to these people, when you become rich and prosperous, the dangers of walking away from God become higher. Therefore, it is better not to have too much money because the money and all the good things that money can buy will cause you to become lukewarm. Eventually, you will start worshiping these things and forget God, who gave you them in the first place.

Then there are those who believe that God wants us to prosper, just as our soul prospers. These people measure God's blessings by the number of houses, fancy cars, jets, boats, gold watches, and all other material things a person has amassed.

The majority of people who believe that believers can prosper also believe this wealth can be acquired through faith. This involves paying tithe, sowing seed, first fruit offerings, and other monetary offerings. The emphasis is on ensuring that these seeds are sown in the right fields for maximum productivity. While these so-called prosperity preachers who collect this seed money can flash fancy watches, clothes, houses, and planes, etc., as proof that the seed sowing Gospel works, most of their followers have little to show.

While it is evident that he who is collecting the money will accumulate more over time, the givers are blamed for not prospering because they do not have enough faith or have not obeyed to the fullest. The givers are not failing to prosper because they do not have enough faith. The issue is that those who are sowing the seed-faith are not wise. Like all other things in life, money is governed by laws and principles. Therefore, if you want to prosper, you must learn what money is, how it works, and how to acquire it.

This book will focus on the fallacy of sowing seed money and expecting the money will grow. God is not a casino! Those teaching that you can sow money in the offering basket or in some ministry and reap a hundredfold return are deceiving their followers. They cannot use their lifestyle to prove that their mischaracterization of the Gospel is true.

Televangelist Benny Hinn has confessed that the excess of the prosperity Gospel has to be checked. According to him, he used to believe and teach that you can sow money seed and reap more money. While some were happy, a prominent preacher like Benny Hinn was finally calling the prosperity preachers out. Others were not so excited because they wanted to keep the people of God in bondage.

The reaction to Benny Hinn's confession has been mixed. Those who hold that prosperity and material possessions are excesses that believers should not be bothered with were excited. According to them, anything to do with prosperity is a no-go zone. They are throwing out the bathwater and the baby.

This book will be making the connection between obeying the greatest commandment, fulfilling the Great Commission while prospering at the same time. It is not about greed and love for mammon and material comforts. Can I add here that many unbelievers are prospering without the Gospel? These people have identified a human need or problem and are meeting it or providing solutions. As long as we live on this earth, there will always be human needs, and those who provide solutions will be rewarded financially.

In this book, I will be making the strong case that loving God and loving our neighbor as ourselves will make us prosperous. This is not some "name it, claim it" Gospel. It is a call to identify your giftedness, develop it, and deploy it. There are no shortcuts, and it will take time and hard work to get there.

Too many people have turned Christianity into another religion. Our Lord Jesus Christ did not die to establish a religion. He spoke all the time about the kingdom of God being established among us. God will not charge us with the instructions to establish His kingdom and not give us the resources to get that done. It is important to understand that all the legitimate wealth created is tied to exploring, exploiting, and developing natural resources that God has created. Millions of different products have been manufactured from these natural resources that God made. These products facilitate the distribution of goods and services and drive economic transactions on a global scale.

God already knew that we would need crude oil to put in our cars; that is why it was created in the first place. He also knew that we would need iron ore to make steel for the car frame, lithium for the batteries, aluminum for planes, potash for fertilizers, etc. How can exploring, developing, and exploiting crude oil and selling the oil be a bad thing? How can using potash to make fertilizers and grow abundant food be a bad thing?

This book will not be your typical book on money and how to get rich. There are tons of such books out there if that is what you are looking for. This is a book about God's involvement in wealth creation and how the people of God should position themselves to be partners with God in expanding His kingdom here on earth.

All I ask of you is to read the book with an open mind and let the facts speak for themselves. There will be many scriptures to back what I am saying, and I strongly encourage you to read them. I hope that after reading, you will no longer fall prey to all these fake preachers and avaricious wolves in sheep's clothing. Instead, you will position yourself to prosper just as your soul prospers. Let us get into the book!

Chapter 1

Why I Wrote This Book

This book attempts to address an issue that has been troubling me for many years. I have pondered this issue in my heart for a long time and think this is the time to put it in writing so that other people can benefit. Nothing breaks my heart more than seeing people living in poverty and misery. The worst part is when the people of God are not living to their full potential because they are being taken advantage of by those who claim to be their leaders and spiritual parents.

This is not a get-rich-quick book and should not be read as such. If you want to prosper, you must learn what God is doing and what you are supposed to be doing. Many are poor and broke because of the misguided idea that all they have to do is give, and blessings will fall from heaven. The days of manna are over! Anybody teaching you to give or sow seed in exchange for some financial increase is deceiving you if the person does not teach you how to work for the increase.

The question of how we got here is the subject of another book. For now, we will focus on what is going on and how to get out of this sinking boat. Teaching people half-truths about money and how money works has caused much pain, disillusionment, and misery in the body of Christ. This has to stop, and the sooner, the better. While there is a place to talk about the dangers of the love of money, it is essential first to discuss the dangers of the lack of money and a faulty understanding of what money is and how it works.

A few years ago, I was invited by a friend to attend a revival meeting in the Dallas area. This friend told me that a powerful man of God who had prophetic powers was the person who would conduct the meeting. According to this friend, this man had the solutions to many different problems because he had the ability to see you for the first time and tell you what you were going through.

I had just arrived in the United States on a student visa and was experiencing many financial difficulties. I could not work off-campus because of my visa status. If a miracle could happen and resolve all these problems, that would be great.

My friend, too, had come to the US to study some years before me but had overstayed his visa and now needed a miracle to resolve his immigration status and joblessness. This friend had a family to support, and things were tight financially. Therefore, he was desperate for a solution. Anything that promised to resolve his problems and relieve his pain was welcomed. He was seeking a solution. In fact, both of us were looking for solutions, and our situation had made us vulnerable to manipulations and deception.

This is the vulnerability exploited by many who claim to be servants of God and to be speaking on God's behalf. These so-called men and women of God knowingly or unknowingly exploit vulnerable people by making outlandish promises that have no backing.

In the case of this Ghanaian prophet, I was shocked by what I saw and heard at the revival meeting. The prophet asked people to sow a seed before praying for them for their problems to disappear. He promised that if they sowed a seed of money, by this time next year, money would appear in their bank accounts.

Then the prophet said something that will remain with me till I depart this earth. He said the man of God did not have a seed, but whoever gives seed to the man of God to sow would have a double reward. The prophet asked the congregation to go home and prepare this special seed for the man of God and come back the next day.

The next day, we came, and some people had brought money to give this prophet to sow. I sat behind and observed in disbelief, and I was dumbfounded that people could be so gullible. I kept wondering why this prophet could not sow his own money if he believed that the money would be multiplied. Why did he need other people's money? Why was nobody raising an objection to what was going on here? How could they let this charlatan get away with this crock?

I am calling this guy a charlatan because of the bizarre things he did in the name of God. He asked people to return home and write down the names of all their enemies, and it should be a list of all the people they suspect may be the cause of their financial issues or whatever problems they may be facing. He instructed the congregation to write these names, buy an olive oil bottle, and bring both with them the following day. I refused to buy any olive oil and did not write any names.

When we arrived at the service the next day, the instructions were even more bizarre. All those who had brought a list and a bottle of olive oil were asked to come out with them. Many people stood up and went out. They were then instructed to put the list into the olive oil bottles. I watched as the people frantically opened their oil bottles, folded up their lists, and inserted them in the bottles.

The bottles were closed and handed to the prophet, who prayed and declared that all whose names were in the bottles should die. With the help of his aides, the prophet then took the oil bottles out to the dumpster and broke them.

The prophet and his aides did the part of breaking the bottles, so I do not know if this next part is true or not. The prophet came inside and informed us that he could hear people shouting and screaming when the bottles of oil were being broken. Then he declared that people should stay tuned because, in a few days, they would receive the news of the deaths of whoever had been blocking their progress. These people may have been uncles, aunts, cousins, parents, etc.

I could not believe what I was hearing and watching. We were in a Christian church, and this prophet was using the Bible to twist and manipulate the people to part with their hard-earned money. When I tried to raise any objection, my friend could not see anything wrong with what the prophet was doing.

My friend was in for a rude awakening because the man of God deceived them to sow their rent for that month with the expectation that the money would suddenly appear in their account. They obeyed and gave their rent for that month. Then, when the time came for them to pay their rent, there was no money, and they almost ended up on the streets.

Psalms 23 for $23 and Isaiah 53 for $53

While I was still processing what was going on, I turned on the TV, and somebody claiming to be a prophet and evangelist said that anybody who sends in $23 would receive the blessings of Psalm 23. What in the world are the blessings of Psalm 23? Are they telling me that these blessings stayed locked until the invention of the dollar? Will these blessings also work with 23 pounds sterling, 23 Euros, 23 Naira, 23 Yen, 23 Yuan, etc.? How do people come up with such "revelations"? Is there any precedence and evidence that those paying the $23 are receiving this blessing?

Then somebody turned it a notch higher by asking for $53. I have actually watched some renowned televangelist in the US request $53 for the Isaiah 53 blessing. According to these individuals, this is some new revelation that explains how to get breakthroughs. While there is freedom of expression and speech, it seems, when it comes to the things of God, that those running these radio and TV stations should caution against such excesses. But it seems they are partnering with these people to fleece money from the people of God.

The givers are hoping to tap into the anointing that the man or woman of God is carrying because they have been taught to believe like that. It is sad that the free access of all God's children to the resources of their Father is restricted by other people. This is an issue that must be addressed, and it is part of the reason this book was written.

Those placing these restrictions may not even be aware of what they are doing, but this is not an excuse for the issue not to be addressed. It is unfortunate that those who preach against the love of money are the first ones to collect money from other people. Where do they think this money is coming from? This is a question that must be asked because the impression one gets is that earning money is not as spiritual as being in full-time ministry or serving God. Jesus said we could not serve two masters. Therefore, we have to choose between God and mammon, yet how this command is interpreted and has been interpreted has far-reaching implications.

This is another issue that this book is going to address. Was Jesus saying that earning money was equal to serving mammon, or was there more to it than what we are being taught? Jesus could not have been against money when He had a money bag and was supported financially by some women. I think Jesus was referring more to an attitude of the heart toward money and how we conduct ourselves when acquiring money. This will be addressed later.

Tried the gimmicks and got no results

The gimmicks of putting money in the offering plate and sowing seeds so that the money can multiply do not work. I am very aware that some will reject this book, and I will be accused of heresy or wrong doctrine.

My challenge to you, the reader, is to do your due diligence and not take my word for it. If you want the truth, you must do your own research. Before you discard this book, make sure that you do a more in-depth study of some of the issues discussed here. You might have been raised in a particular way, and any new information will make you feel uncomfortable and threatened. But the truth is that those who grow are students; they are learning and continue learning until the end of their lives.

Unfortunately, many are quick to defend these excesses even when they are the victims. I often wonder if it is foolishness or a lack of understanding. Please understand that the purpose of writing this book is not to pull down anybody or settle any scores because there are none to be settled. My main goal is to proclaim the truth and let the chips fall where they may.

I used to believe that you can sow a seed of money and harvest money. I mean, you literally put your money in the offering plate or invest it in some ministry with the hope that God will bless you with a great deal of money. While an undergraduate student, I remember emptying my pockets and giving all the money I had because the man of God who was preaching said that sowing a seed would bring forth a good return. The question that was never addressed was how this blessing would come about. This is a question that we will be addressing later.

I obeyed and gave it many times, and it did not work. You may accuse me of being of weaker faith, but I am not the only person who has followed these instructions and ended up in disappointment.

The purpose of this book is to set the record straight. We are not to serve mammon either in or out of the church. This is something that we will dive deeper into in the following chapters of this book.

I encourage you to read to the end before you draw your conclusions.

Somebody has to speak up

Some people have spoken up against the excesses of the prosperity Gospel, and rightfully so. That said, I have an issue with those who talk against prosperity and try to paint poverty and lack as spiritual virtues. This approach is wrong because it shows a lack of understanding of what money is and how it works. It is not enough to say that the role of the church is just the Gospel, yet every Sunday, the offering plate is passed around for a collection. Where is the money to be collected coming from? How was this money made? If money is so evil, why do we need it to spread the Gospel?

People are being hurt

If the current teachings were delivering what they promise, there would be no need for this book at all. The issue is that after more than three decades of being a sincere and faithful follower of Jesus Christ, I am deeply troubled by where things are and what is going on financially. In my book *God's Supernatural Agenda: 7 Steps to Lasting Wealth and Prosperity*, some of these issues were raised and addressed. But here, we will be focusing solely on the mechanics of money and how to earn and grow it.

There are no scores to be settled here, and no attempt will be made to call names or paint anybody in a bad light. This book is an attempt to shed some light on this vexing problem. While it may be a vexing problem to those who have sown money year in and year out without anything to show for it, those who collect the money do not see it as a problem. Who will blame them? They are at the receiving end, and as long as they get the money, it is the givers who have to figure out why the formula is not working for them.

I am making the assumption that those who teach these doctrines have good intentions and sincerely believe that they are helping the people learn how to prosper. Unfortunately, having good intentions is not good enough. A lack of knowledge, understanding, and wisdom will destroy the people.

This is what is happening in the body of Christ. Many people are struggling financially, not because of any fault of their own. Their lack of financial literacy can be traced back to the teachings they have received over the years.

Consider the case of my friend who gave his rent money to the man of God so that he could pray for his condition to change. My friend ended up more destitute than he was previously and was almost kicked out of his house.

Poverty is not decreasing

Instead of making people well off, this type of Gospel that focuses on people giving, praying, and waiting for manna to fall from heaven makes the poor poorer. It is scandalous to tell somebody in debt, poor and broke, to bring money to be prayed for so that it can break their poverty curse.

There is a cure to the curse of poverty: providing goods and services to solve problems people face. This is not the solution that many want to hear. They want shortcuts to instant wealth. If this is what you are looking for, sooner or later, you are going to fall prey to unscrupulous scammers parading in the name of God. These people will make false claims and twist scriptures to say what they want. Their intention is to collect your money and keep you poor.

One of the stories used to insist that even if you are poor, you must first give to the man or woman of God to guarantee your increase is the encounter between the prophet Elijah and the widow at Zarephath:

> Some time later the brook dried up because there had been no rain in the land. Then the word of the Lord came to him: "Go at once to Zarephath in the region of Sidon and stay there. I have directed a widow there to supply you with food." So he went to Zarephath. When he came to the town gate, a widow was

there gathering sticks. He called to her and asked, "Would you bring me a little water in a jar so I may have a drink?" **As she was going to get it, he called,** "And bring me, please, a piece of bread."

"As surely as the Lord your God lives," she replied, "I don't have any bread—only a handful of flour in a jar and a little olive oil in a jug. I am gathering a few sticks to take home and make a meal for myself and my son, that we may eat it—and die."

Elijah said to her, "Don't be afraid. Go home and do as you have said. But first make a small loaf of bread for me from what you have and bring it to me, and then make something for yourself and your son. For this is what the Lord, the God of Israel, says: 'The jar of flour will not be used up and the jug of oil will not run dry until the day the Lord sends rain on the land.'"

She went away and did as Elijah had told her. So there was food every day for Elijah and for the woman and her family. For the jar of flour was not used up and the jug of oil did not run dry, in keeping with the word of the Lord spoken by Elijah. (1 Kings 17:7-16 NIV)

Elijah made a request that made no sense at all. How on earth could he ask a widow to give him her last source of food? This was an unreasonable request, and one could even say that it was inhumane. Even after this woman told Elijah she was pressed to the wall, he insisted she used all she had to make bread first for him before her and her child. What on earth was Elijah thinking, and why did he keep pushing this poor widow?

The answer is not complicated. Prior to this encounter, Elijah was at a brook, and ravens brought him bread. Then the brook dried up, and God specifically instructed him to go and meet this widow for food. The key is that God sent the prophet and promised him that this widow would provide food during this time of famine. Let me repeat: God sent the prophet with *specific* instructions. Elijah did not just come up with this idea.

How many people claiming that the poor should hand over their last dollar for it to multiply have heard from God? Did God ask them to collect money so that the giver can experience an increase?

These questions are being asked because there are people who teach that since they are "men and women of God" - just like the prophet Elijah - you will experience supernatural increase if you give them the little you have. Just like this lady did, and her little oil and flour did not run out.

While the prophet asked that he be the first to eat the bread, it is worth noting that this widow and her son benefited immediately and immensely once he ate the bread made from the little oil and flour that was left in her house.

Unfortunately, today the money only goes in one direction. Those collecting are getting richer, and those giving are getting poorer. Unlike the widow, who was able to benefit from the increase, these days, the money stops with the receivers. This is not strange because it is expected to be so. The only issue is that those collecting are not telling the givers the whole truth.

Suppose those collecting and asking for financial seeds to be sown for the supernatural increase and financial breakthroughs are honest. In that case, they will empower the givers and equip them to provide goods and services because that is how money and wealth are created.

Wolves in sheep's clothing

Jesus Christ Himself warned us about wolves in sheep's clothing:

> Beware of false prophets, who come to you in sheep's clothing, but inwardly they are ravenous wolves. You will know them by their fruits. Do men gather grapes from thornbushes or figs from thistles? Even so, every good tree

> bears good fruit, but a bad tree bears bad fruit. A good tree cannot bear bad fruit, nor *can* **a bad tree bear good fruit. Every tree that does not bear good fruit is cut down and thrown into the fire.** Therefore, by their fruits you will know them. (Matt. 7:15-20 NKJV)

There are many wolves in sheep's clothing posing as men and women of God. Just like wolves, these people are leaving much destruction wherever they go. Therefore, it is imperative to warn God's people to be on the watch for these false teachers and prophets.

God sacrificed His only son for the salvation of the world

When you listen to the admonishing of those trying to collect money to do the work of God, they come across almost as if God has run out of resources. It seems we are the ones funding this supernatural agenda of God. What these people fail to understand is that the God who created the universe was able to sacrifice His only son, and there is nothing more valuable than God's son. Have we forgotten that all the silver and gold, the earth, and all that is in it belongs to God? Then how can all these things that God made become difficult for God to access?

Do we have all this confusion because instead of applying wisdom and understanding to learn how money works, we are approaching it in a manner that is not sustainable? All you need to do is turn on the television or listen to the radio and hear the televangelist talk about the need to collect money and do God's work as if God has run out of money.

I read a quote the other day that caught my attention. The writer was sarcastic, in my opinion, but what the person said is worth examining. This person asked the following question: "Why is it that when the Christians need money, they are asked to go to God, but when the pastors need money, they come to the Christians?"[1] In other words, the pastor should live out their message by going directly to God as the Christians do.

The point I am making here is that God already sacrificed His son without our input, and right now, He will provide financially if we are willing to understand how money works and obey the laws of money. We already obey many other laws. For example, we eat because we will die if we do not eat for an extended period. Nobody in their right mind would pray for their hunger to go away while there is food available to eat and satisfy the hunger. It is

---

[1] Why do pastors ask us to pray to god for money, but when they need money they come to us? (n.d.). Quora - A place to share knowledge and better understand the world. https://www.quora.com/Why-do-pastors-ask-us-to-pray-to-God-for-money-but-when-they-need-money-they-come-to-us

absurd to suggest that anybody would think they can demonstrate their faith by not eating and praying their hunger should disappear.

This book was written to address some of the financial absurdities that pass in the name of faith. There are laws that govern money, and this book will be addressing them. One of the Cardinal Laws is "Thou shall not serve money or mammon."The other one is "Thou shall not love money." The third one is "Thou shall not worship money." Others include "Thou shall not live for money, thou shall not honor money, thou shall not hunger and thirst for money, and thou shall not slave for money."

It is important to understand the difference between the love of money and earning money. Unfortunately, in their zeal to warn others against the dangers of the love of money, many people end up throwing out the baby with the bathwater. While they preach against the ills of money, they turn around and ask for people to give money to support the work of God.

Collecting money is not a complete picture

The other thing that this book will be addressing is the notion that it is more profitable to collect money than to make money. This will be one of the most controversial statements I will make in this book. There are those who are going to hate me for making this statement. They will accuse me of being stingy and against giving to support the work of God and meeting the needs of the needy. Would you hold your fire and read in between the lines before passing any judgment?

How does collecting money from people week after week make them wealthy? Of course, these people show up for a service and are expected to pay for it. If that is the case, the people should have a say in how much they pay for the service. Unfortunately, this is not what the people are told.

Week after week, they are told that collecting their money is going to make them somehow financially well off. If this promise were followed by a concrete way for the people to make money, there would be no problem at all. If it is good to collect money to support the work of God, it is more excellent to make money to support the work of God. Making money is more profitable because, in the process of making money, more people are helped. This book will be diving into this in the following chapters.

What is the work of God?

What is the work of God? This is another important question that needs to be addressed because of its pivotal place in the finances of the people of God. We have been taught all along that a few have been called to do the work of God, and the majority are in an auxiliary and supportive role. This is a convenient and commonsense arrangement. After all, every religion has its clerics, priests, temples, and religious services. A few have been called from among the people to take care of the rest.

This arrangement may make sense, but it is not necessarily what God has sanctioned. Our Lord Jesus Christ did not die to establish a religion. He died to establish the kingdom of God among us. The kingdom operates differently from a religious institution. The Protestant Reformation was ignited by the understanding that for the kingdom of God to be established, the priesthood of every believer has to be established. Therefore, the work of God is not limited to a few people dispensing the sacraments to the majority. All the people are equipped and empowered to do the work of the ministry. This involves sharing the Gospel, discipling the people, and meeting their needs.

The work of God is to love God and love our neighbors as ourselves. When we love God, we will spend time in His Word to learn about Him. As we study the Word, God will speak to us. Then we will, in turn, speak to God through prayer. Through the Word and prayer, we get closer to God as our minds are renewed and transformed. As we deepen our knowledge and understanding of God's nature, we will know what is important to God. It will not take long for us to realize that God sent His one and only son to come and die for our sins. The mission of our Lord Jesus Christ was to rescue, redeem, reconcile, and restore mankind back to fellowship with God. What we lost in the garden of Eden is being restored. In the garden, there was no lack of any sort.

When we realize that God loves people and wants them to be rescued, redeemed, reconciled, and restored, we will get behind this supernatural agenda of God. We will start living the second part of the Great Commandment to love God and love our neighbors as ourselves. Because we love our neighbors, we will share with them the greatest news ever. The love of God in our hearts and the fact that we, too, have experienced what it means to be rescued, redeemed, reconciled, and restored will compel us to share with other people.

How can we say we love people and still keep such great news from them? There are only two reasons: maybe we have not experienced the goodness of God or do not know how to share this great news. The ability to communicate is secondary because when we experience something this important, life-changing, and with eternal ramifications, we will not be able to sit on it without sharing it with those we love. When we eat at a good restaurant, we are not ashamed or bashful to tell our friends about the place, the food, and the exceptional service. We even go ahead and encourage our loved ones to experience this great place with us.

In addition to sharing the greatest news ever with people, we will also care about their well-being. As long as people are living on the earth, certain things need to be cared for if we want the body and spirit to be together. People need food, clothing, and shelter. In addition to these basic needs, people will have to be educated in many areas to reach their full potential. Taking care of people's basic needs requires infrastructure and many other things.

I hope you are beginning to see where I am going with this. What I am saying is that an extension of the love of people is meeting their needs by providing solutions to their problems. These solutions can be in the form of goods and services. While the spiritual is paramount, the physical must be catered to if we want the body and soul to be in synergy.

Therefore, the work of God is not limited to preaching the Gospel alone. It is taking care of the physical and spiritual needs of the people. And all God's people have been called and ordained by God Himself to be major players in doing this. Without a proper understanding of this fundamental truth, people will fall prey to those claiming that they are closer to God or have more of God than the rest of us. When the Bible says that our bodies are the temple of the Holy Spirit who is dwelling in us, it does not categorize (see 1 Corinthians 6:19).

We do not have enough room here to expound on the priesthood of every believer, but there is a lot that has been written on that subject, and I strongly encourage you to research it. At the end of this book, you can find some related resources I have written in this area. Get them and expand your knowledge and understanding. There is only one priesthood, not a priesthood within the priesthood of every believer.

Giving for spiritual and financial breakthroughs

People are sick and tired of false promises and giving money to be prayed for in exchange for promised miracles and financial breakthroughs. There is nothing wrong with giving money to other people and to those preaching the Gospel. But to tie this giving to the idea that the giver will somehow make more money is a gross misrepresentation. Many scriptures are used to support this teaching, but most of these scriptures are not being interpreted correctly. If you teach people that giving their money will make them prosperous but fail to show them how, you are lying to them.

This is just like telling somebody who is hungry to pray, and their hunger will disappear permanently. Nobody does this because we know that when you are hungry, you eat food. While it is possible to go for many days without food, it is not sustainable to have a long life without food.

Even Elijah, the mighty prophet who could call down fire from heaven, had to rely on ravens for food before God sent him to the widow for food. After the famine, while Elijah was fleeing from Jezebel, God woke him and asked him to eat because he had a long journey ahead. On three separate occasions, God did not take away Elijah's hunger or make him not be hungry perpetually.

Don't get me wrong: God has the ability to do anything. That said, He created the world, and there are certain laws that govern how the world operates. Living and operating within these laws is not a sign that we do not trust God or depend on Him. God is the creator of everything, and He is the one who has wired us in a particular way. Therefore, we honor God when we operate and function as He designed us. We do not need to prove a point to anybody by trying to circumvent the laws that God has put in place in an attempt to prove the miraculous. Just being here is a miracle already. This is not ruling out the occasional supernatural or miraculous intervention by God.

There is a place for the supernatural and the miraculous, but we must ensure that things are not taken out of context. When the devil asked Jesus Christ to perform a miracle and turn stones into bread to satisfy His hunger, Jesus refused (see Matthew 4). The request by the devil for Jesus Christ to perform a miracle came with a condition. It was not about the miracle; it had to do with Jesus proving that He was the son of God. But Jesus did not need to prove to the devil that He was the son of God. That is why even though Jesus refused to perform this miracle, He performed many other miracles later on because it was the right context and motive.

Giving for spiritual breakthrough is misguided because it is done out of context. Jesus performed many miracles to bring breakthroughs in many lives, and nobody was required to give anything. The apostles did the same, and nobody was asked to give. The only instance when somebody tried to give money to receive the Holy Spirit was seriously frowned upon. We will be looking at that in greater detail later on in the book.

There is no secular-spiritual divide

Many people believe in the spiritual-secular divide and accept it as the way things are, but the Bible does not teach this secular-spiritual divide. One of the main reasons this book was written is to address this spiritual-secular divide as it relates to money and how money works.

The first error that many make is believing in the secular-spiritual divide. According to those who hold to this idea, the spiritual is superior to the secular. Therefore, making money is presented as a secular activity with almost zero spiritual significance. I often wonder why an offering plate is passed on Sunday to collect this mammon to do the work of God. If money was so evil, why would we need this evil substance to do good? If the time spent in making money was not being maximized for the glory of God, why bother?

If making money is a less desirable or worthy activity, why do we use the money to do the work of God? The questions can go on and on, but I will stop here. The point I am making is that having a distorted view of what money is and is not is at the root cause of poverty, lack, and wasted potential in the body of Christ.

It is important to understand that you have one life. As we will see later in the book, whatever we do, we have to do it unto the Lord. Our activities honor God when we engage in these actives in fear of God. In other words, we do whatever we are doing with integrity and honesty and with no malice, anger, jealousy, hatred, etc. We allow the fear of God to lead and guide our conduct. Whatever we do, as long as it is in line with the Word of God, is going to honor God when it is done in righteousness. That is why you cannot cheat, lie, defraud, and oppress people if you are walking in obedience.

Some think that the end justifies the means. These are people who are driven by pragmatism. To them, as long as it works and delivers the desired results, they will do it even when their action is contrary to the Word of God.

The idea that prayer can be used for money laundry permeates this insistence on the spiritual-secular divide. While those who promote this do not see it this way, their actions reveal their real intent. They hold that making money may be an unholy, secular activity, but when the money is brought to the church and prayed over, it sanctifies the money and makes it fit to do the work of God.

No wonder some Christians separate their Christianity from their money-making activities. They believe that there is no point in incorporating Christianity in every area of their lives. According to them, church attendance, reading the Bible, and praying is enough to make you a good Christian. This is why emphasis is made on attending church programs and going through religious activities, but little is said on how to live out the Christian principles in everyday life.

Don't buy into the idea that God will bless you if you give to support His "work" no matter how you got the money. There are too many people stealing, lying, and cheating, then giving the money in church and expecting a blessing. These are the individuals who say things like, "It is business, and we have to do it the way other businesses are." They fail to understand that they are children of God firstly and must be honoring God, not just in their business transactions, but in all other areas of their lives.

Financial illiteracy is dangerous

The cost of being financially illiterate is enormous. Unfortunately, many spiritualize their lack of understanding of how money works by quoting scriptures out of context. "Blessed are the poor," you hear them say. Yet these same people are working for people who know how money works and have created a job for them to earn money. There is a vast difference between the love of money or obsessing about money and being financially literate.

Those who are financially literate understand that spending more than you make is not a good idea. These people understand compound interest and delayed gratification. When they earn money, they set some aside and put it to work for them by investing the money. These are people who have disciplined and conditioned themselves not to consume to please other people or to fit in.

In the United States of America, 1% of the population controlled 38.6% of the country's wealth in 2016.[2] The politicians keep talking about the increasing gap between the rich and the poor. Some of them are proposing that the wealth gap be bridged by redistributing the wealth. This is a solution that is appealing to the masses because they will be receiving something free. These politicians do not talk about the toll of financial illiteracy that has kept many people trapped in poverty.

Nothing is said about an educational system that does little to educate students on how money works. The emphasis is on getting get good grades and a good job after graduation. By the time some of

---

[2] Matt Egan, "Record inequality: The top 1% controls 38.6% of America's wealth," CNN, September 27, 2017,https://money.cnn.com/2017/09/27/news/economy/inequality-record-top-1-percent-wealth/index.html

these students have graduated college, they are in so much debt that it will take them many years to pay it off. These students are so indebted that there is no breathing room for them to save money, invest, and eventually get out of poverty. The excess borrowing by students is something that could be avoided and minimized, but it is not because most of the students are clueless about borrowing and how interest rates work.

Another thing these politicians do not talk about is that a majority of the top 1% of the families that control most of the wealth of the country are business owners. The politicians don't ask why business owners earn more money than the general population.

It is easy to blame the business owners for being greedy and exploiting those who work for them. While some business owners exploit their workers and do not pay them fair wages, there are those who pay their workers well. Yet, the workers are not wealthy because of financial illiteracy. They are comfortable with their pay and always look forward to the month's end for their check. The drive to get more and be more is misdirected and misguided.

I heard a story by Rabbi Daniel Lapin that speaks volumes about settling down for a salary. He had worked all summer as an intern for a company, selling ceramic wear for them. His internship was in Europe, and they had knocked on numerous doors during the internship to sell their wares. At the end of the internship, the owner called them into a room.

When they were all seated, he gave them two options for employment and subsequent earning of money.

The first option was that he would pay them a base salary each month, and they would also make a certain percentage of whatever sales they made for the month. They were going to be making something like fifteen or so percent in addition to the base salary.

The second option was strictly commission-based, and they would make fifty percent of whatever they sold.

Rabbi Lapin thought for a moment and pondered upon which option to choose. The first option made sense because you were "guaranteed" base salary whether you sold something or not. But you were limited by how much you could make on commissions.

As the rabbi reflected and pondered upon the situation, he had an epiphany. It occurred to him that while the first option was secure because he was guaranteed a base salary, if he was not good at selling, there was no point in him being in the selling business at all. In the long run, if he did not sell successfully, the company would go out of business because it depended on them making sales.

The second option was an excellent choice for those who were good at selling because the more you sold, the more money you would make. In short, you were in charge of how much you could earn.

He chose the second option. The owner asked them to hand over the pieces of paper on which they had written their choices. He proceeded to separate the interns into two groups and sent them to two different rooms. Then he walked into the room with all those who had chosen the second option and congratulated them for making it into the company. The first group was sent packing. The owner explained to them that he did not want to work with people who were not ambitious.[3]

How many people work in jobs because of the "guaranteed salary"? These people put in just the bare minimum to prevent them from being fired. They think that they are smart, but the truth is that they are the cause of their financial poverty. This type of attitude is driven by a total lack of financial literacy.

What to expect

I hope you have not been spooked by some of what you have already read. The rest of the book will focus on developing some of the ideas and questions raised, providing solutions and answers to these questions. To get the most out of this book, you should put on your thinking hat and make sure you read the scriptures, connecting the dots for yourself.

While the tone may appear to be bashing some particular beliefs, it is not my intent to put anybody

[3] Lapin, R. D. (2014). Business secrets from the Bible: Spiritual success strategies for financial abundance. John Wiley & Sons.

down. My main motivation is that the people of God should prosper holistically.

It is easy for those having three square meals a day and living in secure and prosperous countries to pontificate about the benefits of poverty. Most of the world lives on less than two dollars a day, even though every continent is blessed with tremendous natural resources and great human capacity. God will not come down from heaven and do what we have been created and positioned to do. God is the one who gives us the power to acquire wealth, but it is our responsibility to go out there and earn it. We must do the hard work involved in getting wealth. Are you ready to do your part and be all God created you to be? Then let us dive into the book and keep learning.

Chapter 2

First Things First

No one would remember the Good Samaritan if he'd only had good intentions; he had money as well.

—Margaret Thatcher

This book is about money, and therefore, it is crucial for us to start by looking at what money is and what money is not. A few weeks back, I had a conversation with somebody on LinkedIn who was not very happy with my book titled *God's Supernatural Agenda: 7 Secrets to Lasting Wealth and Prosperity.* According to this individual, if I were truly a godly person, I would be focusing on preaching the Gospel of salvation and helping people go to heaven instead of talking about worldly things. Here is how our conversation went, unedited:

LinkedIn Connection: Hi Sir, are you a prophet?

Me: Yes, I am. Why do you ask?

LIC: What verse talk about your ministry?

Me: Matthew 28:18-20, Ephesian 4:11-12

LIC: So, you are a pastor, not a prophet... based on the scriptures you have shared. But you should teach people how to go in heaven and not insisting in lasting wealth

Me: Who made the wealth? The streets of heaven are made of gold, and the foundation stones are gemstones. If you read the book, you would not make the conclusion that you have made. Jesus taught us to store our treasures in heaven where the moth, rust, etc. cannot get there to destroy it.

Do you collect an offering in church? Where does the money come from?

LIC: I insist John the Baptist, Jesus-Christ himself, Paul, Martin de Lourdes, Colomban, Martin Luther, John Wesley, and William Branham have not insisting in material wealth but in Heaven one...Sin is growing and is being stocked at Hollywood where "lasting rich men live" and It should be better if you are a true PASTOR not A so called Personal Development Coach, to preach the repentance and the forgiveness of sins. God bless you

Me: What is a true pastor? If you read my books, you will understand what God has called me to do.

LIC: I respect God servants, so I don't want to last our exchange. **I am a poor and happy to be a "lasting rich in Jesus-Christ"**

Me: My brother, let it be unto you according to the measure of faith. It was nice having this exchange with you.

LIC: (Gave me a thumps up)

Note: Emphases have been added.

Many years ago, I thought exactly the way this person was thinking. My understanding of money and how money works were influenced by my upbringing and the leaders I looked up to. There was also some sort of sneaking suspicion about the rich. The assumption was that amassing wealth is associated with being dishonest, greedy, and somehow compromised in some acts of ungodliness.

Godliness, in our understanding, was to preach Jesus and Him crucified, plus the forgiveness of sin. The believers were heaven-bound, and there was no need to waste time on earthly things. Jesus was going to come back soon, and all should be done to save as many souls as possible. The earth is the devil's playground, and there is no need to waste time doing anything in the devil's territory.

We thought those who are prospering right now are doing so because they are compromised. They are somehow in agreement with the king of this world, the devil, and this explains why he has given them great riches. These individuals have exchanged their souls for material and worldly things.

Why did God send Jesus to come and die?

Different people have different definitions of what the Gospel message is, what we should be preaching, and how to go about it. What matters is not our denominational doctrinal position or church traditions. It is essential to let the Word of God speak for itself. We should use the Word of God to lead us and not just our experiences and preferences.

When God created the cosmos, cumulating in the creation of Adam and Eve, He said everything was good. Then He made a provision for them to eat and have a good time. God is not against us fulfilling the very needs with which He created us.

For example, we get hungry and tired because we are wired to eat and sleep. We do not have hair on our bodies like animals in the wild. That is why we need clothing and shelter. In addition to having needs, God gave an assignment to Adam to name all the animals. This was a great deal of work. After Adam was done, God decided that Adam needed companionship, pleasure, and emotional support. God went ahead and created Eve for Adam.

Picture Adam and Eve in the garden of Eden with all they could eat and having unbroken fellowship with God. This was a good life! But something went wrong, and this setup was shattered. Our first parents rebelled against God and decided to believe the lies of the devil instead of the truth told by God.

God showed up after the rebellion and called out to Adam and Eve because they were hiding away from Him. Their rebellion had made them realize that they were naked. God set in motion a plan to rescue, redeem, reconcile, and restore mankind there and then. The rest of the Bible is about this supernatural agenda of God.

Before God drove Adam and Eve out of the garden, He did the following: "Also for Adam and his wife the Lord God made tunics of skin, and clothed them." (Genesis 3:21 NKJV)

Please note that after God had provided the promise for a spiritual solution to the sin problem, He also provided for their physical needs. God actually made the first clothing to cloth this naked couple.

Those who insist all we should do is preach the Gospel of repentance are missing part of the mandate. The mission is to rescue, redeem, reconcile, and restore. People have physical and spiritual needs, and it is godly to meet all these needs. Both needs MUST be met!

If you doubt this, take a look at how Jesus started His ministry and what He declared concerning the kingdom of God. We are told that this is how things unfolded at the beginning of His ministry:

> So He came to Nazareth, where He had been brought up. And as His custom was, He went into the synagogue on the Sabbath day, and stood up to read. And He was handed the book of the prophet Isaiah. And when He had opened the book, He found the place where it was written:
> "The Spirit of the Lord *is* upon Me,
> Because He has anointed Me
> To preach the Gospel to *the* poor;
> He has sent Me to heal the brokenhearted,
> To proclaim liberty to *the* captives
> And recovery of sight to *the* blind,
> *To* set at liberty those who are oppressed;
> To proclaim the acceptable year of the Lord."
> Then He closed the book, and gave *it* back to the attendant and sat down. And the eyes of all who were in the synagogue were fixed on Him. And He began to say to them, "Today this Scripture is fulfilled in your hearing." (Luke 4:16-21 NKJV)

Later on, during the ministry of Jesus Christ, He healed the sick, fed the hungry, and forgave sins. This is an indication that Jesus was not only interested in the spiritual but the physical as well. We cannot, in good faith, look at somebody who is hungry and naked and tell them that because their sins have been forgiven, all is well. This is the very thing that James, one of the disciples of Jesus Christ, addressed here:

> What *does it* profit, my brethren, if someone says he has faith but does not have works? Can faith save him? If a brother or sister is naked and destitute of daily food, and one of you says to them, "Depart in peace, be warmed and filled," but you do not give them the things which are needed for the body, what *does it* profit? Thus also faith by itself, if it does not have works, is dead. (James 2:14-17 NKJV)

The admonition here is for us to be practical in our faith. Our faith has to be perfected through our actions. There is a need to be practical. We have legitimate needs that God created in us that must be met. If these needs are not met, the spirit will separate from the body. How then is taking care of the spirit and the body a bad idea?

Many will argue that the spirit is eternal and more important. This is true, but as long as you are on earth, you have to take care of the physical as well. Taking care of the physical involves the exchange of goods and services. In other words, commerce facilitates these exchanges. There is no talk about commercial activities without mentioning money because money is at the heart of all commercial transactions.

What is money?

Before defining what money is, let us talk about what money is not. Money is not secular. Money is not bad. Money is not dangerous. Money is not anti-spiritual. Money does not make you walk in unrighteousness. Money is NOT EVIL. This point cannot be emphasized enough because many believe that money is evil. This explains why they have difficulty associating God and money in the same sentence. Money does not make somebody less spiritual. If money is not evil, what is it?

According to Investopedia, "Money is a medium of exchange; it allows people to obtain what they need to live."[4] In other words, money is whatever medium of exchange people have agreed upon to use in exchanging goods and services. Over the years, many different substances have been used as a means of exchanging goods and services. For example, Rai stones, tea bricks, Canadian Tire Money, Parmigiano-

---

[4] "What Is Money?" Investopedia, last modified June 26, 2019, https://www.investopedia.com/insights/what-is-money/

Reggiano cheese, bottle caps, shell money, Shire Silver, mobile phone minutes, Notgeld, and the 100 quintillion pengo have all been used as money.[5]

Here are other forms of exchange that have been used and are still being used:

- **Bartering** was one way that people exchanged goods for other goods before money was created.
- **Like gold and other precious metals,** money has worth because, for most people, it represents something valuable.
- **Fiat money** is a government-issued currency that is not backed by a physical commodity but by the stability of the issuing government"[6]

Are transactions involving money spiritual in nature?

To answer this question, we must first understand that something can be spiritual but not necessarily religious. Mixing the spiritual and the religious is

[5] Talia Avakian, "The 10 strangest things that have been used as money around the world," Business Insider, April 19, 2016, https://www.businessinsider.com/alternative-forms-of-currency-2016-4

[6] "What Is Money?" Investopedia, last modified June 26, 2019, https://www.investopedia.com/insights/what-is-money/

where the problem lies. Spiritual activities are those that cannot be measured quantitatively. For example, love, empathy, honesty, joy, loyalty, etc. In his book *Business Secrets From the Bible*, Rabbi Daniel Lapin says the following about monetary transactions:

> That relationship between currency and God's favor springs from the Bible and the Hebrew language itself, in which the word for God's favor is *cheyn*. This word, really meaning God's plan for human economic interaction, is not only the etymological origin for the English words coin and gain but also for the Chinese word for coin, *ch'ien,* and similar words in many other languages. The word *cheyn* also serves as the root of the Hebrew word for store or shop, as well as for market-based economy. A store or market is a place for people to interact and make voluntary exchanges, leaving both parties happier and better off than they were before.[7]

There is nothing wrong with exchanging legitimate goods and services between individuals. Let's say you are hungry and need some food to eat. The restaurant owner has anticipated that there will be people like you who will become hungry and need food. This

---

7 Daniel Lapin, *Business Secrets From the Bible* (Hoboken, New Jersey: John Wiley & Sons, Inc., 2014), 31.

anticipation compels them to prepare food for you and many other hungry customers. Your hunger pushes you to look for the restaurant. When you find it, you are happy that you have found a place to eat. It even gets better when the food is served. After you have eaten and are satisfied, you go into your wallet, pull out some bills, and hand them over to the waiter. Those bills might have come from the man whose house you painted that morning. That man is happy to have new paint, you are happy to have eaten, and the restaurant staff is happy to have earned money.

We have all been given unique gifts and abilities to serve other people. There are many needs in the world, and each and every one of us serve each other in one capacity or another when we meet these needs. We, too, have our own needs and depend on other people for these needs to be met.

There is nothing wrong with meeting people's needs and providing solutions to problems that people are facing. Money makes this give and take between other people and us possible.

Therefore, money is neutral and cannot be evil. This does not rule out the fact that people with malicious intent use money to facilitate their evil deeds. For example, money can be used to pay an assassin to eliminate one's enemy. It is possible to use money and corrupt judges to pass wrong judgments. Just because people are misusing money does not mean that money is evil. Are our bodies evil? The answer is, obviously, no! But people use their bodies to do evil things.

As you can see, money is neutral, and it is the grease that oils the exchange of goods and services between people. It is a godly thing to provide shelter, food, medicine, clothing, entertainment, education, counseling, protection, etc., for other people.

The relationship between money and the greatest commandment

This chapter is about first things first: the most important thing to understand is the greatest commandment and how it relates to money. There are those who want to separate money from spiritual transactions. These are those who consider poverty a sign of spirituality, although the Bible is filled with many examples of godly people who were prosperous. We will get back to this later on in the book, but for now, let us look at the greatest commandment and how it relates to money.

We are told that Jesus Christ was teaching somewhere, and one of the teachers of the law came and asked Him a question. The man asked:

> "Teacher, which is the greatest commandment in the Law?"

> Jesus replied: "'Love the Lord your God with all your heart and with all your soul and with all your mind.' This is the first and greatest commandment. And the second is like it: 'Love your neighbor as yourself.' All the Law and the Prophets hang on these two commandments." (Matt. 22:36-40 NIV)

On a separate occasion, another teacher of the law put Jesus to the test by asking the following question:

> On one occasion an expert in the law stood up to test Jesus. "Teacher," he asked, "what must I do to inherit eternal life?"
>
> "What is written in the Law?" he replied. "How do you read it?"
>
> He answered, "'Love the Lord your God with all your heart and with all your soul and with all your strength and with all your mind'; and, 'Love your neighbor as yourself.'"
>
> "You have answered correctly," Jesus replied. "Do this and you will live."
>
> But he wanted to justify himself, so he asked Jesus, "And who is my neighbor?" (Luke 10:25-29 NIV)

These men asked two important questions that all of us should be asking. What is it that I can do to please God, and how can I obtain eternal life? Because when it is all said and done, our focus should be on pleasing God and securing the eternal security of our souls. If our motivation is not to please God, we will fall into the temptation of serving mammon.

The answer our Lord Jesus Christ gave to these teachers of the law must have surprised them a little. The first part of the answer about loving God was something with which they were familiar. But the second part about loving our neighbors must have been a little surprising because, in the encounter recorded in Luke 10:25-29, the teacher of the law asked Jesus Christ who his neighbor was.

This man was not expecting what Jesus Christ would say next because He replied with the famous story of the Good Samaritan, as recorded in Luke 10:25-37. We are told that the teacher of the law wanted to justify himself when he asked about who his neighbor was. Here is how the story unfolded:

> In reply Jesus said: "A man was going down from Jerusalem to Jericho, when he was attacked by robbers. They stripped him of his clothes, beat him and went away, leaving him half dead. A priest happened to be going down the same road, and when he saw the man, he passed by on the other side. So too, a Levite, when he came to the place and

> saw him, passed by on the other side. **But a Samaritan, as he traveled, came where the man was; and when he saw him, he took pity on him. He went to him and bandaged his wounds, pouring on oil and wine. Then he put the man on his own donkey, brought him to an inn and took care of him. The next day he took out two denarii and gave them to the innkeeper. 'Look after him,' he said, 'and when I return, I will reimburse you for any extra expense you may have.'**
>
> Which of these three do you think was a neighbor to the man who fell into the hands of robbers?"
>
> The expert in the law replied, "The one who had mercy on him."
>
> Jesus told him, "Go and do likewise." (Luke 10:30-37 NIV) Emphases added.

Much can be said about this parable, but we are going to focus on the practicality of the solution that Jesus gave. It was shocking that a Samaritan was chosen to act as a good neighbor to the man who had fallen among thieves. This sinner who was not holy enough stands in sharp contrast to the priest and Levite, who were holy people. The priest and Levite loved God and were rushing to the temple but failed to obey the second part of the greatest commandment. They did not see the love for fellow man as an expression of love for God. Well, Jesus Christ came to change this, and He did.

The action of the Good Samaritan was driven by love for the man who had fallen among thieves. He saw a need and moved with compassion to meet it. To meet this need, this man had to risk his own life, inconvenience himself, and change his itinerary. He went out of his way to help somebody who was helpless. This Good Samaritan placed his own life on the line to help a complete stranger. What mattered was that this fellow human being was in need.

When this story is told, many people stop at the act of charity that the Good Samaritan did. Sure, he did an act of charity, but he was a person of means. From all indications, he was not poor because he had a means of transportation and could pay for the cost of housing this man in the inn. He also promised to pay all future bills. Imagine that!

You may be wondering where the connection is between making money and loving our neighbors since, in this case, the Good Samaritan gave his money and resources without expecting anything in return.

Here is the connection: The Good Samaritan had money, which would have been earned somehow. He must have exchanged his giftedness in return for the money that he used in meeting the needs of this man. In other words, the Good Samaritan must have solved other problems for people who paid him for his goods and services.

At the heart of this story is love for others and how that love is manifested practically. It is cheap to say "I love you," but it's costly to show that love practically. Resources are often required to show love. Without love, we cannot claim that we know God.

Here is an excellent passage of scripture that speaks powerfully about the significance of love and the crucial need for us to love one another:

> Beloved, let us love one another, for love is of God; and everyone who loves is born of God and knows God. He who does not love does not know God, for God is love. In this the love of God was manifested toward us, that God has sent His only begotten Son into the world, that we might live through Him. In this is love, not that we loved God, but that He loved us and sent His Son *to be* **the propitiation for our sins. Beloved, if God so loved us, we also ought to love one another.**
>
> No one has seen God at any time. If we love one another, God abides in us, and His love has been perfected in us. By this we know that we abide in Him, and He in us, because He has given us of His Spirit …

> **If someone says, "I love God," and hates his brother, he is a liar; for he who does not love his brother whom he has seen, how can he love God whom he has not seen? And this commandment we have from Him: that he who loves God *must* love his brother also.** (1 John 4:7-13, 20-21) Emphases added.

None of us has seen God, but we can demonstrate our love for God by how we love others. If we do not love others, the love of God is not in us, and we do not know Him. When we love people, we will meet their needs just as the Good Samaritan did. We will love in words and in deeds.

Before you can engage in an act of charity like the Good Samaritan, you must first make some money. Therefore, providing solutions to meet people's needs is a loving thing to do. That is why setting up a barbering studio to cut hair is a loving thing to do. Making yourself available to cut people's lawns is a loving thing. Opening a restaurant to provide food to feed the hungry is a good and loving thing to do. In short, anything in line with God's Word that you do, or a product that is placed in the market to meet needs, is a loving and good thing to do. Money is what facilitates all these good and loving things. Therefore, earning money is superior to acts of charity.

This statement is going to get me into much trouble. Let me say it again: Earning money is superior to acts of charity. What I mean is that without meeting the needs of people and getting money in exchange for the goods and services provided, you cannot do acts of charity. You must first earn money before you can do charity.

Therefore, teaching people how to make money should be a fundamental thing that has to be prioritized. It is paradoxical that those who collect money from others care little about how these people are making money.

In some settings, money is seen as a necessary evil. This is the attitude that makes some people feel that having money is a bad thing because it is a sign of some sort of compromise and a lack of a high level of spirituality.

If you doubt what I am saying, you should tell me how many churches honor the businessmen and -women in the congregation. The emphasis is on the fivefold ministry and the gifts of the Spirit. Those who matter are those who are in full-time ministry. Everybody else is somehow doing a lesser job. Then why collect money from those who are not fully engaged in the kingdom of God to do the work of the kingdom?

Please don't cast stones at me yet. I have not said that people should not give to the church. What I am saying is that part of the greatest commandment is to love our neighbors. We demonstrate love for our neighbors through the goods and services that we render to them. Therefore, those who are out there working hard to meet the needs of other people are doing the work of God.

In fact, these people are the hands and feet of Jesus Christ for feeding the hungry, comforting the sick, cleaning the streets, etc. We should stop making these precious people of God feel as if they are not already in ministry and should leave their "worldly" activities and get involved in godly activities.

This was the thinking of the priest and the Levite. They thought that God was in the temple, and it would be a waste of time to meet this man's needs who was lying helplessly on the road. Their other concern might have been based on the assumption that this man was dead. Therefore, they were concerned about becoming unclean if the man was dead and they touched him. So, they ignored him to stay "pure" as well. They had a preconceived idea of where God was and how to love Him. Most of our churches today are not different from this priest and Levite.

We have our godly community and activities that are centered on keeping us holy and close to God. There is nothing wrong with brethren taking care of each other. But based on what Jesus Christ taught here, the neighborhood has expanded beyond our little circle of comfort. We must get out there and meet needs. We must love in a practical way. We bring the presence of God in everything we do by doing it with compassion, honesty, integrity, and love.

In fact, the fruit of the Holy Spirit is given to us so that we can serve other people well: "But the fruit of the Spirit is love, joy, peace, forbearance, kindness, goodness, faithfulness, gentleness and self-control. Against such things there is no law." (Galatians 5:22-23 NIV)

The fruit of the Spirit is not a medal that we hang on our necks and point out to people to see how mature we have become. The fruit of the Spirit is meant to empower and enable us to serve other people. These people are not just believers; we are called to serve all people.

Imagine running your business or doing your job. Everybody in your city would like to come to your restaurant - or whatever business you are running - because you are patient, loving, peaceful, joyous, faithful, and gentle with your customers. When you have customers who rob you or do you wrong, you express self-control. When you have business transactions with other business owners, and they treat you unfairly, you should exercise restraint in your response by exercising self-control.

This is going to be a greater witness than showing up to church on Sunday morning in your Sunday best and sitting in the pews to go through the motions, then, on Monday morning, leaving the "church thing" at home when you go to work. At work, you might speak and curse like anybody else because you have been taught that spiritual activities are to pray, sing in the choir, be an usher, lead a small group, and be a greeter in the house of God. You think these are the activities that truly matter, and we will be rewarded in heaven for doing these things. So you think you can act however you want at work.

Please stop being religious, and please take the love of God with you wherever you go. We have already seen that we have one life, and the secular and the spiritual need to be merged into a single life.

There is nothing immoral, evil, or wrong in serving other people and being rewarded financially for doing that. Remember that without earning money, you will not be able to give money for the works of charity. Therefore, teaching people about money and how money works is not bad.

This implies that those who collect money from others but do not teach them the fundamentals of how money works and how to make money are not giving them the whole truth.

How is money created?

In the United States of America, there is a big push for the separation of religion and state. This push has led to the effort by some to eliminate any mention of God in the public sphere altogether. This push to eliminate God has not only infested the public sphere; it is in business as well.

But there is another more dangerous, often not verbalized, separation that has dramatically impacted the finances of the people of God. This is the separation of the church and money. It is scandalous to mention the words "church" and "money" together.

In many people's minds, it is a cardinal sin to put God's name and money in the same sentence.

This so-called separation of church and money is rooted in a mistaken understanding of what the church and what money are. We have already seen that money is not evil and is just a medium of exchange.

When the word "church" is mentioned, many people think about the church building. I am referring to the physical structure where the believers meet. The building is just a building—nothing more, nothing less. In the new dispensation, we have become the temple of God, and God is no longer living in buildings made by people. The Shekinah glory of God left the temple and has never returned.

In this new dispensation, the body of Christ is made up of the people of God scattered all over the earth. It is not referring to a particular building in a specific geographical location. This explains why the modern-day church building is not equivalent to the temple that we had in Jerusalem. The presence of God is no longer restricted to specific buildings. The temple was destroyed and has not yet been restored.

Am I saying that we should not build church buildings? The answer is no! What I am saying is that they should be called what they are: church buildings and not God's temple. We, the people of God, have become the temple of God.

I am beating a dead horse here for a reason because the seed sowing preachers have been able to successfully manipulate and fleece the people of

God because that which was dismantled has been reconstructed.

First, they have done away with the priesthood of every believer by reestablishing a new priesthood that gives them special status to release blessings on the people. Secondly, the church building has become the temple of God, where they, the priests, serve.

This is the basis for them to ask other people to sow a seed so that they can release a blessing on the seed and make it multiply. Giving money to them ensures that this money will be blessed by God because they are closer to God and have special powers to facilitate this transaction.

If you do not follow this logic carefully, you will not understand why it reached the point where some expect others to bring their money for them to bless and multiply it. What those collecting this money are saying is that they belong to a special class and have been empowered in a unique way to bring down supernatural blessings on those who bring their money to them to be blessed.

You will wonder why people can be so gullible to the extent that they part with their hard-earned money without a second thought. This is a complicated issue because some of those who are being fleeced genuinely want to please God. These people want to walk in obedience and do not want to disobey "God's representatives" on earth.

But there are some who are falling prey because they are greedy. These are those who want to multiply their money with little effort. They are looking for a quick return and shortcut to wealth. These are those who want the money and the good things that money buys. They may claim that they are not greedy and understand how money works. But their ignorance is made evident by them sowing seed money in exchange for an increase.

I have already said that I am not against giving. What I am against is the manipulation done in God's name, taking money from the people of God. The havoc this practice is causing, especially in Third World countries and among the people from these countries in the diaspora, is shocking and very sad. This practice must stop!

Money is created when goods and services are created. If you are not creating goods and services, zero economic activity is being created, and consequently, no money is created. Goods and services are created to meet human needs. Therefore, meeting human needs is one way that money is created.

This implies that collecting money from people and telling them that they will be blessed and prosperous is deceit. The collectors are enriching themselves, and the givers, if not connected to the economy, will not prosper. While people occasionally receive money in their accounts unexpectedly, it is not the norm. If that were how money was created, you who are collecting money from others would have prayed for money to appear in your own bank account.

Of course, the pastor, minister, leader, or whoever is collecting the money understands that money does not literally fall from heaven. They understand that God gives us the power to acquire wealth. And to gain wealth, we actually have to get the work done. This is where faith and work have to meet. Unfortunately, work is hard and messy, and it takes time to get results. This explains why many who collect the money do not want to touch the work portion. They are happy to take the money and let the givers figure out how to earn money.

If you are a leader collecting money from people and encouraging them to be givers, you must also teach, train, and equip them to learn how to acquire the money. This is so crucial, and when neglected, people will live in poverty and lack, but not because they are not paying ten percent of their gross or net income or not giving an offering. People are pounded Sunday after Sunday to give more and sow more seed for prosperity, but little is done in terms of equipping these people and providing seed money for business and other income-generating activates.

It is deceitful to tell people that giving money will multiply it but not teach them how this will happen. If you are interested in collecting, be interested in giving people the necessary skills and resources to earn money.

The idea that we make money and bring it for others to then do the work of God is false. While we are making money by serving other people, we are doing God's work already. Unfortunately, some are wrongly teaching that we make money, which in their thinking is a less noble and spiritual activity, then we bring this money and give it to those who are actually doing the "real work of God" for them to do the work.

The last I checked, the command to seek first the kingdom of God and His righteousness was not given to a select few. We are all charged with seeking first the kingdom of God, and all these other things will be added (see Matthew 6:33). Money and wealth are an addition and not our primary purpose. Unfortunately, the seed-multiplying prophets have made money the most important thing.

Let me repeat myself. The kingdom of God is God, His Word, and people. This implies that taking care of people by providing goods and services to meet their needs is a kingdom thing to do. When you spend time in the Word of God and prayer, you will gain wisdom. As you provide goods and services to other people, money will be added to you. Let us not make it more complicated than this.

Money is not created by sowing dollar bills or putting some coins in the ground and expecting the money to grow and produce more money. This may sound ridiculous, and it sure is. Yet those who advocate for others to sow money in their ministries believe that sending in a monthly contribution or putting the money in will somehow cause whatever is remaining to multiply. HOW? How will this money multiply?

Please don't tell me that it is a spiritual something, and we just have to accept it by faith. Don't forget that I, too, believed this and emptied my pockets into the offering basket and, at one point, was tithing more than twenty percent plus sacrificial offerings. The hope was that my financial situation was going to change based on what I was being taught. It was a lie because the money in my pockets did not overflow, nor did it multiply.

Please don't tell me that God protected me due to the money that I gave and that something worse could have happened to me if I had not given the money. This explanation is a lie because God does not need anything from us to bless us. Remember that Jesus said that God pours rain on both the righteous and unrighteous (see Matthew 5:45). God, too, allows the sun to shine on all people.

Please don't tell me that my reward is in heaven and that I should barely get by at this end. Those who are collecting the money and using it to fund one thing or another, including their lifestyle, will also have a reward in heaven. Why are they tapping into their own reward right now? It is easy to tell other people to volunteer their time and resources for no pay and wait for a reward in heaven while others are paid because they are the called and specially anointed ones. May God help us.

I know this is where many will trash this book and call me a heretic for daring to suggest that all who do the work of God should somehow benefit from it. What is wrong with doing that? I hear that we do not have enough money to pay everybody who works in the church building and other ministries.

You are one hundred percent correct; there is little money to go around. This is the point I am making all along. Who restricted the church from making money? How can making money be a bad idea while collecting is not bad? Why has the church decided to use a welfare module to manage the funds of the people?

It is time to move from collection to talking about how money is actually created. It is blessed to create wealth because it is God who gives us the power to get wealth. Therefore, the people of God should learn how to create wealth by providing goods and services to meet the needs of people. The separation between church and money creation should stop.

Since the pastors may not know how to teach the people of God how to create wealth, they should allow other members of the body of Christ who are gifted in this area to teach other people and help them set up businesses.

Last Sunday, a prayer was made for people who needed jobs. The purpose of this prayer was for the brethren who were not employed to gain employment from other people who, in most cases, are not believers.

If we can pray to God to provide jobs, we can also pray that God will give us the wisdom and ability to run businesses as well. There is nothing wrong with the people of God owning and running businesses. The only thing that can be wrong is owning and running a business in an ungodly fashion. As long as the business is meeting a legitimate need and the operation is done in righteousness, God will honor it.

We have never found any issues with farmers owning and operating farms. We never ask farmers to bring an actual seed in for it to be prayed for so that it can be multiplied without the farmer actually preparing the farm, plowing, planting, watering, weeding, waiting, and eventually harvesting. We know that the increase is in the seed, but the seed has to be planted. The Christian farmer must obey the law of sowing and reaping.

Then why do we treat money differently? There are laws of money as well, and for any increase, the laws MUST be obeyed. Asking people to bring money and sow in the ministry for it to be multiplied is wrong and does not work because it is not obeying the law of money. No wonder most Christians who buy into this fallacy are poor and broke.

One last time! I am not saying giving to support the ministry is wrong. But to give, you must be connected to the economy and obey the laws of money if you want to be blessed. Giving to support ministries and to the poor is just part of the equation. The other part is being connected to the economy. You can either be working for somebody, the government, or for yourself. The best place to be positioned for an unlimited increase is to be using your giftedness to provide goods and services to serve other people.

Who are those who create money?

This may be a very simple question, but how you answer this question will determine how well you will do. Many people have a faulty understanding of this question. This explains why they are poor and fall prey to those telling them to sow a seed for spiritual multiplication.

Those who create money are those who provide goods and services to other people. In short, those who are involved in business activities.

A business is usually set up after a problem is identified. Every legitimate business aims to serve other people by meeting their needs in exchange for their money.

But you may be asking, Why are these goods and services not provided for free? That is an excellent question. The question we should also ask is, Why should the goods and services be done for free? What is wrong with exchanging our goods and services for money or certificates of appreciation, as Rabbi Daniel Lapin likes to call it?

The amount of money in circulation is backed by the goods and services generated in the economy by the people. In other words, money is a facilitator or certificate of appreciation used to help us exchange our goods and services. Money is the grease that enables us to be efficient in serving each other effectively.

God made it in such a way that each and every one of us has unique gifts. The purpose of the gift is to serve other people. You can try to do everything for yourself, but it will be so tiring and almost impossible for you to do it.

Imagine trying to build your own house and car, growing your food, constructing your own roads, building your own bridges, fixing your own teeth, and treating yourself when you are sick. You can throw acting in your own movies in there. You must be saying that this does not make sense.

This is exactly what I am trying to communicate. We need each other. Money facilitates the exchange between all of us. In the past, people tried bartering and realized that this, too, was inefficient.

For example, the farmer who grew wheat needed some chickens because he was too busy growing wheat that there was no time for him to raise any chickens. But this farmer wanted some chicken for dinner. He had to look for another farmer that raised chickens and needed some wheat to make bread. When both got together, they agreed on how many chickens were needed for a bushel of wheat. Then the farmer handed over the required amount of wheat to the chicken farmer, who in turn handed over the chickens to the wheat farmer. Both men parted ways happier because, through their exchange, their needs for that moment had been met.

Without this exchange, the wheat farmer would have gone without chicken for his dinner, and the chicken farmer would have had no bread for dinner. But their getting together made their lives richer.

Assume that in this village was a third party who, instead of doing his own part by growing some vegetables, decided to get up each morning and sleep at home. This farmer refused to work the land and did not plant anything. How would he exchange with other people? Why would somebody give him their wheat, beans, or chickens? This farmer was only a farmer by name and failed to do what farmers do. He was going to starve because, though he was healthy and strong, he refused to do anything. Just imagine if every farmer in that village decided not to do anything. All of them would be poor, and they would all starve because there would be nothing for them to exchange.

This is a simplified explanation of how goods and services are produced and exchanged. The bartering system had many drawbacks because of the limitation of carrying goods around and looking for other people with whom to exchange them.

With time, people decided to use other substances as a medium of exchange. Society agrees that whatever has been selected is legal tender, and this is how money came into existence.

In any economy that is vibrant and doing well, the money in circulation is backed by goods and services that are produced. That is why free is not free. Everybody has to be doing their own part for the economy to function smoothly and efficiently.

When you say that things ought to be free, you are indirectly saying that the farmer who refused to grow any vegetables should be given a chicken. Where will the chicken come from? We all have twenty-four hours in a day, and some of this time is used in producing goods and services to serve others. Without people using their time to produce their share of the goods and services, society will not work.

Imagine living in a city where people do not do their own part of what is required of them. Things will be dysfunctional and will not work.

Next time somebody says free stuff is great, think about productivity and everybody doing their part. Nothing is free! Somebody had to produce it. The government is not supposed to just print money because printing money without it being backed by the production of goods and services leads to hyperinflation. This type of inflation renders the medium of exchange useless.

There is nothing free. Let us go back to the three farmers and assume that the wheat farmer and the chicken farmer decided to take pity on the lazy farmer by giving him some "free wheat and chicken" for a meal. The lazy farmer who refused to work his land will have chicken and wheat for dinner because it cost the other two farmers time and energy to produce his dinner. While the lazy farmer may think that he is smart for not working yet having dinner, he is not aware of the fact that he is just one meal away from starving. Because if the other two farmers do not give him food, he will starve. That is why this lazy farmer must get into contributing his share in the exchange process.

There is a difference between being lazy and not having the ability to be productive. Don't get me wrong. Those in our society who are truly poor because they cannot be productive because of one illness or another should be cared for by those who are strong, hardworking, and productive. But this should be for a season until these individuals can be nursed back to health so that they too can be productive.

If healthy individuals are not working and contributing to the production of goods and services in the country, it will lead to debt. The government will collect fewer taxes, and to pay for all the so-called "free stuff," they must borrow money from other producing countries.

As I write, the United States of America owes more than $27 trillion. [8] This debt is growing at an alarming rate. When you divide the debt by the entire population, each US citizen owes about $69,000. If you divide it by just the taxpayers, they would

---

[8] US Debt Clock.org. (2021, February 8). U.S. National Debt Clock : Real Time. https://www.usdebtclock.org/

owe even more: $186,000. The taxpayers owe more because there aren't as many people producing goods and services, thus paying taxes.

The only way the government will become solvent is by getting more people to produce goods and services. The next thing is to reduce those who are receiving certificates of appreciation (money) for doing nothing. It does not make sense to appreciate people who have not done anything worth appreciating. Yet our politicians move around and promise to do just this. These days there is much talk of free stuff: free health care, free education, free housing, free food, free phones, etc. The fundamental question is, Who is going to pay for all this free stuff?

How does money work?

We can all agree that money does not grow in the soil and cannot be harvested from trees. Although there are some people who believe, talk, and act as if money can be harvested from trees. These are those who erroneously teach that money will somehow miraculously multiply when it is used to support a ministry. They have the audacity to call some ministries a fertile ground and other ministries barren ground.

Those who teach this will argue that they do not literally mean that money will grow if given to a particular ministry. What they mean is that God was going to miraculously multiply the money that is remaining in the hands of the giver. The push to sow money for spiritual breakthroughs and growth is motivated by this faulty understanding.

Just like plant seeds that have laws that govern increase and growth, there are laws that govern how money works. Therefore, it is imperative that anybody interested in growing their money should understand these laws and obey them. It is only after you discover these laws, learn them, understand them, and apply them that you will truly prosper.

We have defined money as a medium of exchange. For this medium of exchange to be used, goods and services have to be produced.

Therefore, for money to grow, goods and services have to be produced. Without any production of goods and services, the money will not grow. While this explanation of how money works appears to be too simplistic, many people do not understand it.

If people did, they would not be playing the lottery and giving their money to other people to pray over it and make it grow. Even when the widow came to the prophet Elisha (2 Kings 4) to help her with the debt her husband had left her, he did not just hand over money to this poor widow to pay her debts. The prophet asked the woman to go home and provide a service to her neighbors by selling oil to them.

This woman experienced multiplication not by money falling down from heaven but by using the little oil that she had to meet the needs of her neighbors, who rewarded her by giving her money.

In other words, this widow provided a product to her neighbors, who happily gave her their money. With this money, she was able to pay off her debts.

It is not uncommon to hear some preachers challenge believers to pay tithes because, according to them, this is how their money is going to grow. These preachers insist that if you are not paying tithes and sowing seeds, you are not trusting that God is your provider. This sounds good until you take a close look at how money works and realize that you will not grow money like this. If you are not connected to the economy and providing goods and services, you are violating the laws of money and will not have any harvest.

We already saw how seeds work. First, you prepare the ground, plant the seeds, and wait for them to germinate, grow, and bear fruit. Then you harvest. If any of these stages are skipped, you will never have any harvest, no matter how much you desire, and even fast and pray for an increase. The increase is in the seed and will be brought out by obeying the laws that govern seed sowing and harvesting.

When it comes to money, you must be involved in producing goods and services. Even when you invest money, you are enabling other people to deliver goods and services. You do this by funding the activities of those in the economy who are actually involved in producing goods and services.

Take, for example, someone who has an idea to make a new brand of tires because the present ones cannot withstand extreme temperatures in the desert. This individual does not have money to fund this idea. He goes to the bank and borrows money that has been deposited by people who earned money through producing goods and services. With this money, this inventor is able to pay those who will work with him to get this idea developed. The bank charges some interest on the loan that is given out to the inventor. Part of the interest is then given to those who deposited their money in the bank.

When you buy shares in a company, you are also putting your money to work because you are enabling the production of goods and services. If there is no production of goods and services, no money will be produced. This is a basic economic principle, and those governments that have violated it by just printing money have landed in much trouble.

That is why counterfeiting any currency dilutes the currency and, in the long run, will ruin the economy if not checked. Counterfeiting is terrible for the economy because it is money that is not backed by any productivity. For those expecting money to multiply without productivity, it will not work because it violates the basic laws of money. You don't create money for the sake of money without it being backed by the production of goods and services.

In some cases, you can grow your money by investing it in land or real estate. After some time, if the economy does well, you can sell the land at a profit. The person buying the land does so happily, and you do not make a profit by extorting money from them.

Therefore, for money to work for you, it is imperative that you produce goods and services with the money you already have. To have enough money freed up for you to put to work, you must delay gratification and learn how to spend less than you make.

The other thing that must be done is to avoid impulsive consumption. This is the type of buying to make yourself feel good, not because you cannot do without whatever you are buying. Some people have a habit of shopping. Immediately after some money gets into their hands, they must go out and spend it all. If they do not spend the money, they will not be happy.

There is good and bad debt. Bad debt is consumer debt. This is borrowing money to eat out or buy a new flashy car or fancy clothes. Those who get trapped in consumer debt will never be wealthy—but borrowing money to invest in producing goods and services, when done correctly, will build wealth.

I remember how I got into buying and selling goods after I graduated from high school. Initially, I did not have much money to get the business going, but I started with the little I had. With time, I gained the trust of the other traders in the city to the point where they would allow me to take goods on credit, go and sell, then come back and pay them for the goods I borrowed. The ability to borrow increased the volume of business that I was able to do.

Some have argued that God's economy is different from that of the world. But they cannot back it with any evidence. When the Bible talks about Abraham, Isaac, Jacob, Job, and all those who are wealthy in the Bible, it also mentions the goods and services that they provided. Therefore, teaching people to sow seed for wealth building is deceiving the people because that money will not grow. People must be involved in providing goods and services to other humans.

If you doubt what I am saying, I want you to look at all the billionaires that we have, the likes of Bill Gates, Mark Zuckerberg, Jeff Bezos, etc. They are all producing goods and services that are serving the population and meeting needs.

The bottom line is that if you want money to work for you, it is imperative that you are involved in producing goods and services that will meet other people's needs. Those who do not want to serve others will remain poor. The reward for caring enough to meet other people's needs is money. With the money, you will have your own needs met as well.

How much money is enough?

This is another wrongly worded question that many people ask. The question should be: how big is your assignment? The size of your assignment determines the resources that will pass through your hands.

If you are providing goods and services to meet the needs of many people, you are going to receive a lot of money or certificates of appreciation. There is nothing wrong with helping people and exchanging the goods and services you are supplying for money.

Some people may be saying that this should be done for free. We have already discussed that the idea of free is counterproductive. You cannot do it for free because there is a cost associated with producing goods and services, and somebody has to pay for that cost.

I do not know how much money is enough, but what I know is that to him that more is given, more is expected (see Luke 12:48). God has given you the ability to acquire wealth, and when you become wealthy, you should allow the wealth to pass through you to others. Don't become a hoarder by holding on to the money and making an idol out of it.

Nobody has the moral authority to tell anybody how much money is enough for them. This is because there is no way you can determine what somebody's assignment is and how they should go about carrying it out.

The best attitude to have is to focus on your own assignment and ensure that you have deployed your giftedness and are using it to provide goods and services to solve problems for other people.

Is poverty a sign of spirituality?

Just because somebody is poor does not mean that they have some special spiritual status. From what we have seen so far, the question should be, Is this person poor because they are not providing goods and services to other people? It has nothing to do with being spiritual or not.

There is an encounter between Jesus and a rich young ruler that some use to justify being poor for the sake of the Gospel. Let us take a look at the exchange between Jesus Christ and this young rich ruler:

> Now behold, one came and said to Him, "Good Teacher, what good thing shall I do that I may have eternal life?"
>
> So He said to him, "Why do you call Me good? No one *is* **good but** One, *that is,* **God. But if you want to** enter into life, keep the commandments."
>
> He said to Him, "Which ones?"
>
> Jesus said, "'You shall not murder,' 'You shall not commit adultery,' 'You shall not steal,' 'You shall not bear false witness,' 'Honor your father and *your* **mother,'** and, 'You shall love your neighbor as yourself.'"

> The young man said to Him, "All these things I have kept from my youth. What do I still lack?"
>
> Jesus said to him, "If you want to be perfect, go, sell what you have and give to the poor, and you will have treasure in heaven; and come, follow Me."
>
> But when the young man heard that saying, he went away sorrowful, for he had great possessions. (Matt. 19:16-22 NKJV)

This young ruler was interested in obtaining eternal life. He was smart enough to realize that human life is temporal and that eternal life is a good thing for which to aim. But his wealth had trapped him. Even though he had kept all the other commandments, his trust was in the wealth that he had accumulated. This explains why Jesus Christ instructed him to sell all he had, then come and follow Him. This man had to choose between trusting Jesus and trusting his wealth. Unfortunately, the rich young ruler decided to choose his wealth. He did not understand the principle of gain through loss. According to him, letting go of everything would have meant eternal poverty for him.

After this young rich ruler left, Jesus said certain things that, if taken superficially, may appear to support the idea that being poor is a sign of spirituality:

> Then Jesus said to His disciples, "Assuredly, I say to you that it is hard for a rich man to enter the kingdom of heaven. And again I say to you, it is easier for a camel to go through the eye of a needle than for a rich man to enter the kingdom of God."
>
> When His disciples heard *it,* **they were greatly astonished, saying,** "Who then can be saved?"
>
> But Jesus looked at *them* **and said to them,** "With men this is impossible, but with God all things are possible." (Matt. 19:23-26 NKJV)

Many people take this passage of scripture to support the idea that being poor is a sign of spirituality. Because Jesus said it was difficult for a rich man to enter the kingdom of heaven and easier for a camel to pass through the eye of a needle, some have interpreted it to mean that if you are poor, it will be easier for you to enter the kingdom of God.

How is it possible that poverty will make it easier for somebody to enter the kingdom of heaven? Salvation is free and is not based on our works. It is a gift from God. Therefore, entering the kingdom of God has nothing to do with our economic status.

This rich man got into trouble because his trust was in his riches. The man could not part with the riches he had. Had he understood that it was God who gave him the power to get wealth, he would have trusted the instruction that Jesus gave to him and obeyed. But the man refused to obey.

There are many people today who do not want to believe in Jesus Christ because they have mistakenly believed that their wealth is all they need. This deception is based on the fact that their money has been able to buy them all that money can buy, and they are having too much "fun" with the money that they have forgotten their creator. You do not need to be poor to remember your creator.

When Peter heard what Jesus said, he was troubled, and that prompted the following discussion:

> Then Peter answered and said to Him, "See, we have left all and followed You. Therefore what shall we have?"
>
> So Jesus said to them, "Assuredly I say to you, that in the regeneration, when the Son of Man sits on the throne of His glory, you who have followed Me will also sit on twelve thrones, judging the twelve tribes of Israel. **And everyone who has left houses or brothers or sisters or father or mother or wife or children or lands, for My name's sake, shall receive a hundredfold, and inherit eternal life. But many** *who are* **first**

> **will be last, and the last first.**" (Matt. 19:27-30 NKJV) Emphasis added.

> "Therefore do not worry, saying, 'What shall we eat?' or 'What shall we drink?' or 'What shall we wear?' **For after all these things the Gentiles seek. For your heavenly Father knows that you need all these things. But seek first the kingdom of God and His righteousness, and all these things shall be added to you.**" (Matt. 6:31-33 NKJV)

From the answer that Jesus Christ gave, He is not against riches because He is promising that those who have suffered loss as a result of the kingdom will gain a hundredfold. We have also been promised that seeking first the kingdom of God and His righteousness will result in all the other things being added. These are the things that money buys.

The rich young ruler was more concerned and worried about the stuff that his money bought for him that he forgot who the true source of the money was. Had he understood that God was the source, he would not have hesitated to sell off everything and follow Jesus Christ.

It is easier for society to think that those who do works of charity are doing more good than those who actually produce goods and services. This is backward thinking because most of those doing charity work depend on those involved in producing goods and services to fund their activities. Then how can those who are funding these activities be doing less good compared to those who are running these funded activities?

Is wealth a sign of spirituality?

This is another question that is simple, yet the answer is not so straightforward. The answer will depend on who is asking it and what they want to achieve. Spirituality means many different things for many different people. But we will answer this question in light of the Christian faith.

In Christendom, there are those who hold that poverty is an indication of being holy. They often use the example of Jesus Christ and the early apostles to support their case. There are many scriptures that warn about the love of money and the dangers of lusting for wealth.

We already looked at the story of the rich young ruler that is often used to support the call to live in poverty. Another story that is also highlighted is that of Lazarus and the rich man (see Luke 16). We are told that Lazarus used to go and visit this rich man, and he would not share his food with him. The rich man instead sent his dogs to go and lick the sores on the legs of Lazarus. When both eventually died, Lazarus went to paradise, and the rich man went to hell.

The other story is that of the rich man who had a bountiful harvest and decided that he would expand his barns and have a great time (see Luke 12). That very night, God demanded his soul. In short, the man died that night.

There are those who warn about the dangers of becoming soft and lax because of the trappings of wealth. What they fail to understand is that Abraham was very wealthy, Isaac too was wealthy, and Joseph was in charge of the entire Egyptian economy. King David was not poor; King Solomon was extremely wealthy; Job, who lost everything, ended up with twice what he lost.

When the wrong questions are asked, the wrong answers will be given. Asking if Christians are supposed to be wealthy is one of the most unfortunate questions. It is a total failure of understanding what money is and how money is made and how money works.

At the turn of the last century, whale blubber was used for heating and in streetlights. Then crude oil was discovered in the ground. This new product has generated millions and created billionaires across the world. The question is, Who made the crude? Who gave the wisdom on extracting the crude from the ground and refining it into different petroleum products?

Who made the diamonds from which the De Beers have made a fortune? What about the iron ore that has been used to make the steel that has been used to build the world economies? The list of questions can go on and on. But the answer is simple. God made everything and gave us the wisdom to extract these earth resources, process them, and meet human needs for shelter, transportation, food, clothing, medicine, etc.

How can using our brains to explore God's resources and processing these resources to meet human needs be a bad thing? If there is nothing wrong with what I have just explained, then wealth is the outcome of using our God-given abilities to explore, exploit, and develop these resources and meet other people's needs.

When we walk with God and are willing to use our God-given giftedness to serve others, we are going to prosper. If you learn the laws of money and obey them, you will prosper. There is no shortcut and no gimmicks to prospering. You will have to identify a need and provide either goods or services to meet that need. When you do this, you are going to reap a financial reward. The money you make in the process is in exchange for the time you invested in providing the goods and services. You will, in turn, take the money and use it to get goods and services from other people.

Therefore, the question is not whether wealth is a sign of spirituality. It should be, Has God gifted us? If the answer is yes, then we should use our giftedness to serve other people in fear of God, and the rest will follow.

When you diligently serve other people, and they give you money, don't act "spiritual" and refuse the money. You have to accept the money and pass it on. Other people who are also providing goods and services need that money. Receive the money and pass it on.

Never forget that it is God who gives you the power and ability to gain wealth, and you are blessed to be a blessing. You fail when you hold on to the money and start trusting it or use the money to commit evil. This is why the love of money becomes the root of all evil (see 1 Timothy 6:10). Those who love money will do everything within their power to get it. For them, it is not about serving other people in fear of God but grabbing as much as possible.

The Ten Commandments of Money

1. Thou shall not serve money or mammon
2. Thou shall not love money
3. Thou shall not worship money
4. Thou shall not live for money
5. Thou shall not honor money
6. Thou shall not hunger and thirst for money
7. Thou shall not covet your neighbor's money
8. Thou shall not lust after money
9. Thou shall not steal money
10. Thou shall not work for money

These ten commandments of money, if obeyed, will keep you out of trouble. You are not going to be worried if you are walking in righteousness or not. It is a befitting way to end this chapter on first things first.

At the beginning of the chapter, I said some people fall prey to charlatans and sheep in wolves' clothing when it comes to money because they have greed in their hearts. If you are disobeying any of these ten commandments of money, you have a propensity to fall prey to those who want to extort you for money.

I hope that you will be wise enough to ask the right questions when somebody, no matter who they are, asks you to give them your money for it to multiply or grow. All you need to ask is, HOW IS THIS GOING TO HAPPEN?

Chapter 3

Money Does Not Grow on Trees

Focus on solving real problems and not on making money. There will be enough takers for your solutions. You will help make the lives of some people better, and money will follow. — Bhavish Aggarwal

If you know where the money tree is, please, I would like the directions to the place. I remember a conversation I had with myself and God and the devil when I first came to the US as a graduate student. Before coming to the United States, I was a graduate student in Cameroon, my country of birth, going to school without any thought of moving to the US to continue my studies. Then I attended the 2001 Geologic Society of Africa (GSA) international conference in Yaounde.

During the conference, while the keynote speaker was delivering his speech, I heard clearly in my spirit that it was time for me to leave Cameroon for the US for graduate school. The issue with this command was that it was financially impossible for me just to get up and move to the US for graduate school. I left the conference with this idea in my mind, wondering how it would come to pass.

When I got home, I told my wife that God was asking us to move to the US and that we were going to pray our way there. I think we understood the power of prayer because we had prayed our way to marriage. I proposed to her while I was in my first year as an undergraduate student. I was poor and broke, yet I told her that if she gave me four years, we would get married. That was in 1996. This explains why we got married on December 31, 2000. There was no way the four years were going to elapse without us getting married. We had overcome all odds.

After just three months from this faith walk that had taken us four years, God was stretching our faith once more. This time around, it was more than our wildest imagination. It would require about 75 million CFA Franc[9] or more for me to go through a Ph.D. in the US. This is a conservative estimate based

[9] Ministère de l'Europe et des Affaires étrangères. (2021, February 8). Franc zone. France Diplomacy - Ministry for Europe and Foreign Affairs. https://www.diplomatie.gouv.fr/en/country-files/africa/franc-zone/

on the exchange rate at the time. While this figure may seem far-fetched, my immediate concern was that we did not have even one hundred thousand in the bank that we could use to get the process started.

I needed to take the Graduate Record Exam (GRE) and Test of English as a Foreign Language (TOEFL); it would take me two years of meticulous saving to raise the money required to register for those exams.

In short, we were poor, very poor, and there was no way I was able to do this on my own. This is how a little more than a year after this idea of traveling to the US was dropped in my spirit, I found myself in the US with no money.

I grabbed a single suitcase with a few clothes and borrowed money from money lenders at ten percent a month. This was a whopping 120% a year. Some people have asked me if this was even legal. I don't know whether it was legal or not. Have you heard about payday loans? These are loans that target the poor and those in financial crisis. While the average interest on credit cards is 15%-30%, debt management programs are 8%-10%, personal loans are 14%-35%, and online lending is 10%-35%, the average payday loan is 391% if it is paid in two weeks—if not, the interest can be as high as 521%.[10]

---

[10] "How Do Payday Loans Work?" InCharge Debt Solutions, accessed October 29, 2020, https://www.incharge.org/debt-relief/how-payday-loans-work/.

These types of high-interest rates targeting the poor and people who are already in financial distress do not look right. I am not here to discuss the merits and demerits of predatory lending. This is a discussion for another day.

What I am driving at is the fact that if you are poor, in need, and do not know how money works, you will fall prey to money lenders and predatory lending practices. The simple reason is that you are vulnerable. When a lion looks at a herd of deer, it does not attack the healthy and strong ones. The lion picks out the weak deer and goes behind it. While this is not good for the deer, it is good for the lion because it provides lunch for it.

I had borrowed money, and the interest was $300 a month. While this may be a small amount, it was a massive mountain before me when I had just arrived in the US as a graduate student who was not earning a dime. At that time, the exchange rate was 756.23 FCFA for each dollar[11]. This means that I was expected to pay 756.23*300 = 226,869 FCFA. This amount was mind-boggling to me because about two

[11] "Treasury Reporting Rates Of Exchange," U.S. Department of Treasury, accessed October 29, 2020, https://www.govinfo.gov/content/pkg/GOVPUB-T63_100-fab63240b6208a926bd391a4d87ad4e2/pdf/GOVPUB-T63_100-fab63240b6208a926bd391a4d87ad4e2.pdf

years prior to moving to the US, I had difficulties paying my monthly rent of 2,000 FCFA.

As I was contemplating this mountain of debt before me, I heard the devil taunting me about the debt. I was made to understand that I was on my own and would never get out of the debt. The devil asked me why God did not throw the money down from heaven or put it in a big bag and place it under my bed. The conclusion was that there was nothing I could do and that God had failed me because the money I needed had not just appeared suddenly. The mockery was relentless, and my faith was being taunted and ridiculed. The enemy was asking me if I had such great faith, why did I not command the money to appear so that I could pay my debts?

There was no point trying to argue with the devil because he was making some points by pointing out that the money had not fallen down from heaven and that it had not appeared in my room. I told my Heavenly Father that the idea of coming to the US was His own, and since He had not thrown down the money from heaven but allowed me to borrow, He owed it, and it was now His responsibility to pay off the debt. After saying that prayer, the taunting stopped, and I had my peace. But I did not know how or when the money was going to be paid. It would take a couple of months to sort things out. You can read more in my book *Coming to America: A Journey of Faith*.

I thank God for this experience and the lessons it taught me. This book has been motivated by that experience. If you have never fasted because you do not have anything to eat, it may be difficult to understand the pain and stigma that poverty carries. This does not mean that you have to do crazy things to earn money to get out of poverty. It just means that a proper understanding of money and how it works is imperative.

Money does not grow on trees. Therefore, you cannot harvest money from any tree. You can harvest fruits from a tree and sell them for money. But to harvest the fruits from the trees, they must first be planted by you or somebody else. Therefore, there is a process involved, plus time, seasons, and work.

Those teaching that sowing a seed of money can multiply it are trying to circumvent this process. Unfortunately, they are breaking the laws of money. No wonder people sow their seeds, year in and year out, name and claim, yet they remain poor and broke. Life is governed by laws. Those who understand these laws and live by them will prosper. If you decide to "spiritualize" and refuse to obey the laws that govern money, you are going to remain poor and broke. *No matter how much $1,000 seed you sow, you will remain poor if you are not loving God and loving your neighbor by providing goods and services to meet their needs and serve them.*

Therefore, instead of sowing monetary seeds, you should be planting actual seeds and waiting for the trees to grow and bear fruit. Then you harvest the fruits and meet people's need for nutrients and vitamins. The people will give you money in exchange for your fruits. This is just one way that you can make actual money and not some pie in the sky money that you will never get.

If sowing seed for financial breakthroughs were something we could count on, we would have eliminated world poverty a long time ago. This idea is a fallacy and does not work. Those who push this may be unknowingly deceiving people, but for the most part, they know they are exploiting the greed, laziness, and ineptness in people.

Those parting with their money have allowed their greed, impatience, and lack of diligence to blind their eyes. They want money and want it now! They are willing to circumvent and break the laws of money with impunity. But they fail to understand that we do not break laws, but laws break us.

If you break the laws of money, you are going to be poor. Don't let anybody deceive you that your faith is not strong enough and that you failed to keep all the commandments, and that's why you have been sowing seeds of money yet remain poor.

But with faith, all things are possible

You cannot wish your way to earning money. It is impossible to circumvent the laws that govern money and prosper. I can hear some of you telling me that those who walk by faith can do and undo. Well, you are seriously mistaken. Even Jesus Christ Himself, when He was tempted by the devil to jump from the top of the temple to show that He was the son of God and that God was with Him, refused to do a miracle. The devil had rightly quoted scripture to buttress his demand for Jesus to prove that He was the son of God:

> Then the devil took Him up into the holy city, set Him on the pinnacle of the temple, and said to Him, "If You are the Son of God, throw Yourself down. For it is written:
> 'He shall give His angels charge over you,'
> and,
> 'In *their* hands they shall bear you up,
> Lest you dash your foot against a stone.'"
>
> Jesus said to him, "It is written again, 'You shall not tempt the Lord your God.'" (Matt. 4:5-7 NKJV)

The devil knows the Word of God very well and can quote it exactly as well. Here is the portion of Psalm 91, which he quoted to try and deceive Jesus Christ to act presumptuously and put God to the test:

> Because you have made the Lord, *who is* **my refuge,**
> *Even* the Most High, your dwelling place,

> No evil shall befall you,
> Nor shall any plague come near your dwelling;
> **For He shall give His angels charge over you,**
> **To keep you in all your ways.**
> **In *their* hands they shall bear you up,**
> **Lest you dash your foot against a stone.**
> You shall tread upon the lion and the cobra,
> The young lion and the serpent you shall trample underfoot. (Psalm 91:9-13 NKJV) Emphases added.

The devil took scripture and quoted it out of context, trying to cause Jesus to put God to the test. Unfortunately for the devil, Jesus Christ was by far smarter than he thought. Jesus Christ understood the law of gravity and did not want to break it. By the way, there was no need for Jesus Christ to prove to the devil that He was the son of God because Jesus knew who He was. Jesus was living by faith and did not need an external miracle to prove who He already was.

For you to put your money in the collection basket and expect the money to multiply because, according to you, it is a seed that you have sown by faith, it is putting God to the test. If I were you, I would not do it. You are falling into the trap of the enemy and testing God. You cannot circumvent the law of money by giving and not working. Money is created, as we have already seen, by producing goods and services. Therefore, giving alone will not bring about increase and prosperity. In addition to giving, you must work. In other words, it is imperative that you are providing goods and services to meet the needs of other humans. This is how money works and grows.

Money will never be thrown out of heaven to you because it is in violation of the principle of providing goods and services to meet the needs of people. There are too many scriptures that talk about the dangers of laziness and how this leads to poverty. Therefore, if you are told that an increase will come your way if you just sow a seed of money, you should run away.

All the wealthy people, including some of the prominent billionaires, are business owners. Those who do not directly run businesses are investors. In other words, they are using their money to support those who are providing goods and services. This is what permits them to share in the money that is generated.

It is, therefore, not a sign of faith to sow a seed of money and expect it to multiply; it is being foolish and acting on presumptions. No wonder many people have followed this advice and have sown money year in and year out and are still to reap any return. The person collecting the money can show that they are prosperous by their fancy cars, houses, and expensive clothes.

This is not strange because these individuals are actually collecting money from the people. They are providing a service through the word that is preached. But for those who support them to prosper, they must be providing their own goods and services.

If you are not providing any services, yet you expect a financial increase, you somehow believe that money grows on trees. Since money does not grow on trees, you will be disappointed and eventually disillusioned because your money will never multiply, no matter what you have been told. You can pray and fast all you want and demonstrate your faith all year; it will not work.

No farmer in their right mind keeps their seed at home, prays over it, and expects the seeds to multiply. The farmer prays for the seeds that he has planted because the increase stored in the seed only comes out when the seed is actually planted in the soil, watered, cared for, and allowed time to do its work.

If any farmer were to tell us that he will plant his seed in some ministry because it is fertile ground, then wait for the increase, we would say that farmer is crazy. Don't get me wrong; I believe in the supernatural and also believe that God is the creator of everything. That is why I do not take the increase that comes from planting a seed and waiting for it to yield fruit for granted. Some people may say that this is a natural phenomenon and should be expected. In other words, God is not involved in the process.

For your information, God is involved in the process of a farmer sowing seed and having a harvest. How else can we explain how a seed was designed to be planted in the ground, and out of it comes a tree, which eventually produces fruit? And who provides the conditions for its growth? Here is what the Bible has to say about what happens in farming:

> The Lord will open to you His good treasure, the heavens, to give the rain to your land in its season, and to bless all the work of your hand. You shall lend to many nations, but you shall not borrow. (Deut. 28:12 NKJV)

> Then He will give the rain for your seed
> With which you sow the ground,
> And bread of the increase of the earth;
> It will be fat and plentiful.
> In that day your cattle will feed
> In large pastures. (Isaiah 30:23 NKJV)

God is involved in every aspect of the process and should be glorified for sending the rain and, eventually, the increase. We do not need to miraculously pray for seeds in our pantry to multiply for us to prove that God is involved in the process. The law of increase in the seed was put in place by God Himself because He is the creator. Therefore, there is no need to ask that God somehow miraculously prove a point to us.

Building wealth is not something that we do apart from God because He is the one who gives us the power to get wealth. To make money, goods and services have to be produced. These goods and services at times are produced by exploiting and processing resources that God created:

> In the beginning God created the heavens and the earth … Then God saw everything that He had made, and indeed *it was* very good. So the evening and the morning were the sixth day. (Gen. 1:1, 31 NKJV)

> In the beginning was the Word, and the Word was with God, and the Word was God. He was in the beginning with God. All things were made through Him, and without Him nothing was made that was made. (John 1:1-3 **NKJV)**

> The earth *is* the Lord's, and all its fullness,
> The world and those who dwell therein.
> For He has founded it upon the seas,
> And established it upon the waters. (Psalm 24:1-2 NKJV)

> Eat whatever is sold in the meat market, asking no questions for conscience' sake; for 'the earth *is* the Lord's, and all its fullness. (1 Cor. 10:25-26 **NKJV)**

God created EVERYTHING and declared that it was good. Then He created mankind in His image and likeness. This explains why only humans have the ability to create goods using the materials that God created.

Therefore, we do not have to wait on God to come and do what we have already been equipped to do. God has created the raw materials, and now it is our turn to use these raw materials to create goods and services to meet the needs of people by solving their problems.

What is wrong with doing things? How is this somehow a mundane activity that does not have spiritual merit? Was it not God Himself who charged us to work? How can working become something that does not fall under a "spiritual" pursuit?

Here is why God created mankind and what He assigned them to do after they were created:

> Then God said, "Let Us make man in Our image, according to Our likeness; let them have dominion over the fish of the sea, over the birds of the air, and over the cattle, over all the earth and over every creeping thing that creeps on the earth." So God created man in His *own* **image; in the image of God He created him; male and female He created them.** Then God blessed them, and God said to them, "Be fruitful and multiply; fill the earth and subdue it; have dominion over the fish of the sea, over the birds of the air, and over every living thing that moves on the earth." (Gen. 1:26-28 NKJV)

> The Lord God took the man and put him in the Garden of Eden to work it and take care of it. (Gen. 2:15 NIV)

We're charged to have dominion over the earth and to rule over everything. Then God placed the resources for us to make things and gave us the brains to make this happen. This explains why we have been able to extract various resources from the earth, transform them, and dominate the land, air, ocean, and even outer space.

In the course of carrying out this divine mandate, many different goods and services have been produced, and this production is exchanged between different people through the help of money.

We are back where we started. Money does not grow on trees, and it is not a sign of being super spiritual for you to wait for God to double your money because you sowed a seed.

If you want to multiply your money, obey the first mandate, and that is to have dominion over the earth and to rule over it. You do this by producing goods and services. If you are not producing any goods and services, you are waiting to harvest money from a tree. This is never going to happen, and the result will be poverty.

Chapter 4

The Law of Sowing and Reaping

You're frustrated because you keep waiting for the blooming of flowers of which you have yet to sow the seeds. — Steve Maraboli

There is a law of sowing and reaping, and those who obey it will reap the benefits. This law is not a respecter of age, size, geographic location, or socioeconomic status; it is a universal law that works everywhere. But for the law to work, it must be understood and obeyed to the letter. This law does not take into consideration how people feel or what their preferences are. You cannot circumvent this law without being hurt in the process. Therefore, it is prudent to study this law, understand it, and obey the law. When you obey this law, you are going to prosper.

Unfortunately, the law of sowing and reaping has been distorted by many to mean what it is not intended to mean. The misinterpretation of this law prompted this book to be written.

It is, therefore, crucial that you pay close attention to this law and make sure that you understand how it works and how to obey it. When people disobey laws, the penalty that is embedded in the law breaks these people. Consider a child touching a hot stove; their hand will be burned by the stove because hot stoves should never be touched with bare hands. The stove is not mean and wicked. The blame is not on the stove because it is doing what it was designed to do, that is, to produce heat that will cook food. The child got burned by the stove because the child used the stove for the wrong purpose.

There are cases of poverty that can be traced to somebody breaking laws of increase and wealth building. This is not to talk down to the poor but to say that if something is broken, it can be fixed. You may be born poor, but staying poor becomes a choice. If your parents disobeyed laws, you must not follow in their footsteps; you can choose to take a different path. This is not easy, but it is doable. I am glad that you are reading this book. There is always a way out for those who are willing to seek help.

Because the law of sowing and reaping is such a powerful law with far-reaching implications, it has been abused and misinterpreted a lot. The result is some of the abuses and excesses that are being done in the name of God. Here is the famous scripture that many people quote to justify this distorted view of sowing money:

> Do not be deceived, God is not mocked; for whatever a man sows, that he will also reap. For he who sows to his flesh will of the flesh reap corruption, but he who sows to the Spirit will of the Spirit reap everlasting life. And let us not grow weary while doing good, for in due season we shall reap if we do not lose heart. Therefore, as we have opportunity, let us do good to all, especially to those who are of the household of faith. (Gal. 6:7-10 NKJV)

The passage is definitely talking about how we live our lives with regard to the actions that we take. Sowing in the flesh is allowing the love of the world, lust of the eyes, and the pride of life to direct our actions. Those who live like this are more concerned about what feels good and brings them momentary satisfaction than following the Word of God. While you may feel good momentarily by "following your heart," you will, in the long run, reap the negative consequences that are associated with living in disobedience to God. You cannot break the law of God because the law will break you. There are negative consequences embedded in the law, and those who violate the law will suffer those consequences.

But Isaac sowed and harvested a hundredfold

When I was still young, I read the interpretation of Isaac sowing and reaping a hundredfold that categorically stated that if we sow money, we will harvest a hundredfold. I was too young and unknowledgeable to question this teaching. Therefore, I believed it without any reservation. All I needed was to give sacrificially above my tithe and offering. No wonder I paid a twenty percent tithe and emptied all the money that was in my pockets in the offering basket because I wanted to be blessed. I did all this because I love God and desired to please Him by walking in obedience. The thought of not obeying what I was being taught did not cross my mind.

But I was not going to remain an infant for life; this explains why I am witting this book. Over the years, my eyes began to open as the Holy Spirit began to reveal truths in the Word of God that had never been taught to me. I began to have doubts and questions regarding some of the teachings that I had grown up hearing.

Let us take a look at the story of Isaac and see what happened. The story goes as follows:

> There was a famine in the land, besides the first famine that was in the days of Abraham. And Isaac went to Abimelech king of the Philistines, in Gerar.

> Then the Lord appeared to him and said: "Do not go down to Egypt; live in the land of which I shall tell you. Dwell in this land, and I will be with you and bless you; for to you and your descendants I give all these lands, and I will perform the oath which I swore to Abraham your father. And I will make your descendants multiply as the stars of heaven; I will give to your descendants all these lands; and in your seed all the nations of the earth shall be blessed; because Abraham obeyed My voice and kept My charge, My commandments, My statutes, and My laws." (Gen. 26:1-5 NKJV)

Prior to this famine, another famine in the land forced Abraham to move down to Egypt. While in Egypt, Abraham had to lie about his wife in order to make it there. Maybe this is part of the reason God told Isaac not to go to Egypt when famine struck again. But what we know is that there was a famine, and God told Isaac to stay put and not move to a different location. Egypt was the most powerful nation on Earth at that time, and it made all the sense for Isaac to move there for greener pastures. Maybe other people were doing the same thing, yet God placed an injunction on him not to go to Egypt. Isaac obeyed, and here is what he did:

> Then Isaac sowed in that land, and reaped in the same year a hundredfold; and the Lord blessed him. The man began to prosper, and continued prospering until he became very prosperous; for he had possessions of flocks and possessions of herds and a great number of servants. So the Philistines envied him. Now the Philistines had stopped up all the wells which his father's servants had dug in the days of Abraham his father, and they had filled them with earth. And Abimelech said to Isaac, "Go away from us, for you are much mightier than we." (Gen. 26:12-16 NKJV)

Isaac did not try to solve the famine problem the way others were. Because he chose to obey God and sowed seed, God blessed him. Isaac understood that the increase was in the seed and that if he were living in obedience, God would bless him no matter what his physical environment was.

There is no mention here of any money. Therefore, Isaac could not have sown money. He planted physical seeds. This is what God blessed. This implies that to tell people who are in poverty because they have not been producing goods and services that the only way to get out of their poverty is by planting a monetary seed is a deceit of the highest category. Isaac had received specific instructions from God to stay put. Then he obeyed the law of sowing and reaping. He plowed the ground and planted seeds. There is no magic that Isaac performed to get this increase.

Those teaching that people in economic distress, debt, and financial difficulties should sow a seed for multiplication are misquoting this scripture and misleading the people of God. They fail to understand that Isaac was obeying specific information from God and that his actions did not violate the law of sowing and reaping. Isaac did not try to circumvent the process. He planted the seeds in the midst of the famine and waited for the seeds to germinate and produce.

Why would anybody be told that their debts will suddenly disappear if they sow a seed of money? How will this debt disappear? It is unfortunate that many people still fall for this. The simple reason is that they lack a proper understanding of how money works and how money is created.

Without the production of goods and services, there is no creation of money. Instead of teaching people to sow a seed to get out of debt or poverty, why not teach them how to cut back on their consumption and delay gratification? In addition to taking these measures, people should get involved in producing goods and services. For it is in the production and distribution of these goods and services that they will experience supernatural increase and abundance.

For example, it will make more sense to pray and anticipate God to use your product to meet the needs of thousands, hundreds of thousands, and even millions of people while you put in the work. This is how you experience a hundredfold return when you "sow" in famine. An increase does not come through you sowing money in some ministry. This is not to say that you should not support the ministry, but that you should not be deceived into thinking that this act alone will bring you increase and multiplication.

"But there is a spiritual significance of sowing seed"

You may be saying that there is a connection or spiritual connection between sowing plant seeds and the seed of money. By the way, can I say that there is no such thing as a money seed? This is an invention of those who want to defraud people of their hard-earned money. We have already seen how money is created, and it has nothing to do with seeds. While some may insist that money can be spiritual seeds because plant seeds are physical, they are reading into scripture what is simply not there. To assume that a plant seed is just a physical substance that has nothing to do with God is not taking the whole counsel of God into consideration. God created the plant seed, and the increase in the seed is programmed by God.

Here is another scripture that is often quoted and misinterpreted to mean that God wants and expects us to sow money seeds for massive financial increase. But a close look at this scripture will reveal something entirely different from the interpretations that some are drawing and have drawn from it.

This is an account of what happened after the global flood that led to the death of everybody on earth except Noah's family and all the animals that were in the ark. When the waters of the flood subsided, and Noah came out of the ark, he decided to worship God:

> Then Noah built an altar to the Lord and, taking some of all the clean animals and clean birds, he sacrificed burnt offerings on it. The Lord smelled the pleasing aroma and said in his heart: "Never again will I curse the ground because of humans, even though every inclination of the human heart is evil from childhood. And never again will I destroy all living creatures, as I have done.
>
> **As long as the earth endures,**
> **seedtime and harvest,**
> **cold and heat,**
> **summer and winter,**
> **day and night**
> **will never cease."** (Gen. 8:20-22 NIV) Emphases added.

Noah did an excellent thing by offering a burnt sacrifice to God and worshipping Him for keeping His promise to spare him and his family. The sacrifice pleased God, and He made a promise never to destroy the earth with water again. God also promised not to curse the ground; then, He added that there will always be seed and harvest time.

This scripture talks about planting plant seeds and harvesting the increase that these plants produce. We are told that after the flood, Noah planted a vineyard, and it did so well that he made some wine and drank so much that he passed out drunk.

There is no indication that the promise for seedtime and harvest time has anything to do with money at all. It is about planting seeds into the ground and waiting for the seed to produce fruit. There is no wiggle room here for this to become money, no matter how hard some try to make it about money.

But Paul the Apostle taught about sowing money seed

It is important to read scripture within the context and make sure that you are not reading what you want into the scriptures but allowing them to speak for themselves.

This is easier said than done. Most of the confusion we have is based on the fact that people already have pre-held positions and look for scriptures to defend their positions. This is something that I too may fall prey to, and I am not afraid to say that you should read what I am writing with caution and make sure that you read the Bible passages that have been quoted to make sure that my interpretations make sense.

I do not, in any way, claim to know all the truth or have a monopoly over it. What I am doing here is addressing an issue that I have observed in the body of Christ that needs to be addressed. Some of the passages are pretty long because I want the scriptures to speak for themselves. What I think is not as important as what the scriptures say. The other thing is that many people seldomly read books with the Bible by them to check the scriptures quoted in the book. I figured that it would be easy to include the scriptures so that my readers can read them and make up their minds about what we are discussing.

There was a famine among the brethren in Jerusalem, and Paul decided to collect money to send to the brethren. This is the backdrop of the following passage:

> Remember this: Whoever sows sparingly will also reap sparingly, and whoever sows generously will also reap generously. **Each of you should give what you have decided in your heart to give, not reluctantly or under compulsion, for God loves a cheerful giver. And God** is able to bless you abundantly, so that in all things at all times, having all that you need, you will abound in every good work. As it is written:

> "They have freely scattered their gifts to the poor;
> their righteousness endures forever."
>
> **Now he who supplies seed to the sower and bread for food will also supply and increase your store of seed and will enlarge the harvest of your righteousness.** You will be enriched in every way so that you can be generous on every occasion, and through us your generosity will result in thanksgiving to God.
>
> This service that you perform is not only supplying the needs of the Lord's people but is also overflowing in many expressions of thanks to God. Because of the service by which you have proved yourselves, others will praise God for the obedience that accompanies your confession of the gospel of Christ, and for your generosity in sharing with them and with everyone else. (2 Cor. 9:6-13 NIV) Emphases added.

Unfortunately, when this scripture is quoted by many, they do not mention the purpose for which this money was being collected. The emphasis they give is on sowing a seed so that you can be blessed. Little or nothing is said about giving the money to help the poor, but it is always about supporting an anointed ministry that God is doing great things through. The lure is the idea that God is doing miracles through this ministry, and because of that, whatever money is given will be multiplied.

I am not saying that there is anything wrong with supporting ministry, but we should encourage people to give for the right reasons and with the right explanation.

When some read that God is the person who supplies the seed to the sower, they make people think that money will somehow appear in their bank account. Why would God break the laws that govern money? Any money that is not backed by the production of goods and services is bad money. This explains why some governments just print money, and more money ends up ruining the economy. All you need to do is look at Zimbabwe under Mugabe and now Venezuela. These economies collapsed because of the galloping inflation directly tied to currencies that were not backed by adequate production of goods and services.

You are going to be blessed if you sow in the lives of other people financially and give to different ministries and the church. But money is not going to drop down from heaven, nor will it multiply in your bank account. You will have to be connected to the economy for you to experience an increase. You must be providing goods and services to meet people's needs for you to be blessed.

I am not ruling out the possibility of some other person giving money directly to you. But for this person to give money to you, they might have received it also or are connected to the economy. If you trace the money, it is going to lead you to the production of goods and services. Therefore, if you want to prosper and experience an increase, you should learn about what it takes to produce goods and services to meet other people's needs.

One of the failures of the prosperity preachers is that they do not spend enough time, energy, and resources talking about the need to produce goods and services. The emphasis is only on the giving, and you shall be blessed. The question is how these blessings will come about. Without making provision for the how, people can give all they want and will remain where they are. You do not need to take my word for it; look around and see how many who have been faithful givers over the years but not connected to the economy are poor.

You must sow actual seeds

If you want an increase, it is important for you to understand that faith without works is dead. You have actually to sow seeds and many seeds. King Solomon said the following about sowing seed:

> In the morning sow your seed,
> And in the evening do not withhold your hand;
> For you do not know which will prosper,

> Either this or that,
> Or whether both alike *will be* **good.** (Eccles. 11:6 NKJV)

> He who tills his land will be satisfied with bread,
> But he who follows frivolity *is* devoid of understanding. (Prov. 12:11 NKJV)

> He who tills his land will have plenty of bread,
> But he who follows frivolity will have poverty enough! (Prov. 28:19 NKJV)

Many people who fall prey to unscrupulous preachers, charlatans, and wolves in sheep's clothing do so because they are chasing fantasies. These people want to make manna fall from heaven.

Please don't accuse me of not having enough faith because I am against sowing a faith seed for financial breakthrough. The issue is that sowing seed for financial breakthrough and supernatural increase does not work. It only works for the person who is receiving the money, period! This practice does not work because it violates both the laws of money and faith. Genuine faith is backed by works. For work to be profitable, it has to follow specific laws and principles.

This is why farmers do not keep their seeds in the storehouse and just pray for the seed to multiply. Why should they do this when the law of increase is in the seed? They must plant the seed for it to multiply. Have you ever gone to a service where farmers were being prayed upon for an increase without them actually plowing their fields and sowing seeds? Anybody who did such a thing would be called crazy. Then why is money being treated differently? Why are the rules of money being broken? No wonder many are poor and broke!

If you want some financial increase, you must figure out the laws of money and obey them. We are blessed to be a blessing. That is why we give when we are blessed. While it is more blessed to give than to receive, you must be giving through the production of goods and services. It is not enough to "sow money seeds."

Chapter 5

Give, and It Shall Be Given to You

I give to panhandlers on occasion, especially around the holidays, but have always been involved with charity, which was an important part of the way I was brought up. My siblings and I knew early on in life that we were incredibly fortunate and have never taken that for granted, so we recognize the importance of giving back. — Donald Trump Jr.

When it comes to sowing seed for financial prosperity, nothing is abused more than the concept of "give and it shall be given to you." We are going to take a close look at this and see how it relates to seed sowing and monetary return.

Throughout this book, I have made it clear that I am not against giving. I am a firm believer that for him who has been given much, much is expected. We are blessed to be a blessing. In other words, we have to let the blessings flow through us to other people. Instead of becoming the Dead Sea, which only receives and never allows anything to go through, we have to be a free-flowing river that allows God's blessings to flow through us to other people.

We are living in a fallen world; because of the corruption of sin, people may find themselves in a hard place that will make them unable to produce any goods and services for a season. During this season, they will need some help to get back on their feet. But this has to be for a season, and all should be done to help these individuals to become productive. The secret of walking in abundance is being productive.

Therefore, there is a need for us to give to those in need because God is not going to come down from heaven and take care of our neighbors for us. It is our responsibility to be the hands, feet, and eyes of Jesus Christ to those poor and hurting in our community.

Spiritual vs. secular giving

This is a crucial question that must be answered. I grew up with the understanding that our giving is categorized: there is giving to God and giving to humans. One of the types of giving is more spiritual than the other. In fact, if you want a reward for your money and a mighty return, you must ensure that most of your giving is spiritual.

Here again, we have the spiritual and secular divide. We have already discussed that this divide is arbitrary and is not valid. We are spiritual people and have one life. Everything that we do, we are supposed to do it unto the Lord (see Colossians 3:23).

The secular-spiritual divide when it comes to giving is not biblical. Those who teach that giving to the ministry, or spiritual giving, is paramount and guarantees a return because we are giving to God may have to cut out some scriptures from the Bible that we will look at in a moment.

This teaching is rooted in the idea that doing God's work is the domain of those who have a "special calling" into full-time ministry to do the work. Everybody else is an auxiliary member and is supposed to be a supporter of the main people who are truly doing God's work. All other ministry work is secondary and does not carry equal weight. If your money is not placed in the offering plate and prayed over, you will not be blessed.

All this sounds great, and many people buy into it because that is what they have been taught. But is this true? Can it be backed by scripture? Is there any such thing as a fertile ground that guarantees our money to multiply when we sow in it?

Those who teach that some grounds are more blessed than others may have forgotten the following command from scripture to give to the poor:

> Whoever is kind to the poor lends to the Lord,
> and he will reward them for what they have done. (Prov. 19:17 NIV)

According to this scripture, if you want to give to the poor, you are giving to God.

> There is *one* who scatters, yet increases more;
> And there is *one* who withholds more than is right,
> But it *leads* to poverty.
> The generous soul will be made rich,
> And he who waters will also be watered himself. (Prov. 11:24-25 NKJV)

> Those who give to the poor will lack nothing,
> but those who close their eyes to them receive many curses. (Prov. 28:27 NIV)

It is categorically clear here that we are to give to the poor because it is giving to God. Don't let anybody tell you that if your money is not placed in an offering plate and prayed over, your giving does not count. You should give your offering but not neglect to give to the poor.

This is controversial, and I am going to receive much heat for saying this. But I have to say it because many who teach that the local church is where all ministry takes place also insist that if the money does not pass through the local church, it will not be blessed.

How strange that when Jesus taught about the Good Samaritan, He did not say he was required to go through some unique organization to be a good neighbor. Instead, the priest and the Levite, who were part of the temple and believed that the presence of God was there, missed an opportunity to be good neighbors.

It is no wonder most Christians are ineffective in their witness and are not making any impact in their communities because the "experts" must give their approval for them to be good neighbors. The day of reckoning is coming, and those who have tried to cage the people of God will be asked why they did it.

All the emphasis and efforts to take the church out of the walls to the community are not working properly because of the way things are set up. If passing money through the local church is the only way that blessings are guaranteed, many people would rather jump over a suffering neighbor and go to the local church and give than give directly to the neighbor.

Jesus Christ was more direct about whom to give to

There is a spiritual explanation as to why Jesus Christ was crucified. We know that before He was born, He had already been slain since the foundation of the earth. In short, Jesus was born to die, and He died to forgive our sins.

But the reason why Jesus was crucified also has to do with money and power. The chief priest and religious leaders were not happy when Jesus tampered with the source of income and power.

Jesus Christ was forgiving sins and not charging anything. The multitudes started flocking to Him because His influence was growing by the day. The religious leaders realized that the status quo was changing and not in their favor.

First, if Jesus kept freely forgiving sins, the required sacrifices for the forgiveness of sins would stop coming to the temple. This meant that the choice pieces of meat that the high priest was entitled to would be lost forever. If people stopped going to the temple, the temple taxes would cease, and this source of revenue for the religious leaders was something with which they were not willing to part.

Lastly, people flocking to Jesus instead of the religious leaders meant that they were losing power and control over the people.

Here is what Jesus Christ taught about whom to give to:

> When the Son of Man comes in His glory, and all the holy angels with Him, then He will sit on the throne of His glory. All the nations will be gathered before Him, and

He will separate them one from another, as a shepherd divides *his* sheep from the goats. And He will set the sheep on His right hand, but the goats on the left. **Then the King will say to those on His right hand, "Come, you blessed of My Father, inherit the kingdom prepared for you from the foundation of the world: for I was hungry and you gave Me food; I was thirsty and you gave Me drink; I was a stranger and you took Me in; I *was* naked and you clothed Me; I was sick and you visited Me; I was in prison and you came to Me."**

Then the righteous will answer Him, saying, "Lord, when did we see You hungry and feed *You,* or thirsty and give *You* drink? When did we see You a stranger and take *You* in, or naked and clothe *You?* Or when did we see You sick, or in prison, and come to You?" And the King will answer and say to them, "Assuredly, I say to you, inasmuch as you did *it* to one of the least of these My brethren, you did *it* to Me."

Then He will also say to those on the left hand, "Depart from Me, you cursed, into the everlasting fire prepared for the devil and his angels: **for I was hungry and you gave Me no food; I was thirsty and you gave Me no drink; I was a stranger and you did not take**

> **Me in, naked and you did not clothe Me, sick and in prison and you did not visit Me."**
>
> Then they also will answer Him, saying, "Lord, when did we see You hungry or thirsty or a stranger or naked or sick or in prison, and did not minister to You?" Then He will answer them, saying, "Assuredly, I say to you, inasmuch as you did not do *it* to one of the least of these, you did not do *it* to Me." And these will go away into everlasting punishment, but the righteous into eternal life. (Matt. 25:31-46 NKJV) Emphases added.

This parable clearly teaches that we are to give to the poor and those in need. Jesus made it clear that when we do this, we are doing it unto Him. It must have been unsettling to the religious leaders when He taught these things.

Those teaching that money has to be sown in their ministries for the sowers to be blessed do not like such passages and seldomly preach on them. When they do, they want the money for the people to pass through them and be blessed before going to the poor. This is not what Jesus was teaching here. It is about individual responsibility. What are you as an individual doing for the plight of the poor whom you encounter?

Give to your enemies

If sowing seed as some teach only works when you sow in fertile soil, then the following scriptures talking about giving to our enemies do not make sense:

> Do not repay anyone evil for evil. Be careful to do what is right in the eyes of everyone. If it is possible, as far as it depends on you, live at peace with everyone. Do not take revenge, my dear friends, but leave room for God's wrath, for it is written: "It is mine to avenge; I will repay," says the Lord. On the contrary:
>
> If your enemy is hungry, feed him;
> if he is thirsty, give him something to drink.
> In doing this, you will heap burning coals on his head.
>
> Do not be overcome by evil, but overcome evil with good. (Rom. 12:17-21 NIV)

> If your enemy is hungry, give him bread to eat;
> And if he is thirsty, give him water to drink. (Prov. 25:21 NKJV)

These scriptures clearly teach that we should give to our enemies because it is the right thing to do, and it pleases God. But giving to the enemy is not sowing seed in fertile soil.

If a “fertile soil” is a precondition for God’s blessings, then giving to your enemies and the poor is a waste of seed. Unfortunately, this is how some people think about where and whom to give to. These individuals, in their quest for blessings from God, neglect those who are in need around them. They have been taught that for their money to be blessed, an anointed man or woman has to bless it — no wonder the seed-sowing Gospel keeps spreading, especially among those who are poor and vulnerable.

Give, and it shall be given to you

I kept the best for last. Here is one of the most quoted scriptures when it comes to sowing seed:

> Give, and it will be given to you: good measure, pressed down, shaken together, and running over will be put into your bosom. For with the same measure that you use, it will be measured back to you. (Luke 6:38 NKJV)

The first and most important thing that has to be said about this verse is that it is not talking about money. This was talking about putting grain in a basket or container and shaking it until it spills over. The society that Jesus Christ ministered in was an agrarian one, and they understood what Jesus was talking about when He used this illustration.

This is not to say that we cannot use this admonishment to encourage people to give, but it has to be done within the context of encouraging them to have a generous spirit and to be givers. It becomes problematic when this is used as motivation to sow a seed for financial increase and breakthrough.

We have already discussed that it is more blessed to give than to receive. Therefore, we should encourage people to be givers and not just receivers. But it is disingenuous to tell people that if they sow a certain seed in a particular ministry, they will receive much money in return. This type of teaching may have good intentions, but it is deceptive because that is not how money works.

If you want to experience abundance and increase, identify your giftedness, then develop and deploy it by providing goods and services to people. When you serve other people with your gifts, they will give back to you by paying for those goods and services. Any other way of hoping to get money is building castles in the sky.

Money, as we have already discussed, must be backed by productivity. Therefore, if somebody is promising you a big return on your money but not telling you how it is backed by productivity, you should run.

You may be wondering why this chapter was titled "Give, and It Shall Be Given to You." If you give, it shall be given to you. But if you are giving money and expecting that the money will be multiplied and given back to you, it will not work. The only way your money can grow and multiply is when it is invested in economic activities that are backed by the production of goods and services.

Give because it is more blessed to give than to receive, but if you want to give and experience financial increase, you should give goods and services in exchange for financial compensation. There is nothing wrong with exchanging your giftedness for financial compensation. We have already seen that money is not evil but a means of exchange.

Chapter 6

The Path to True Financial Freedom

The purpose of this book is not to bash those who are wealthy or those seeking to be wealthy. It is to teach you how to improve your finances. When you find a counterfeit, rest assured that there is the real thing around. The fact that people are using draconian ways to try and become prosperous is an indication that there is a right way to be financially prosperous.

Some will argue that Jesus did not die on the cross for us to become financially free. From all that we have discussed so far, it is evident that earning money and being financially prosperous is not sinful.

Instead, if we love God and love our neighbor as ourselves, we are going to prosper. Our objective is not prosperity, but it is to love God and love other people. While this may appear to be too simple, it is the secret of lasting wealth and prosperity. The statement I just made may appear to be a contradiction. How can I say that our objective is not prosperity but say if we love God and love our neighbor as ourselves, we will prosper? I think the answer lies in defining what prosperity is.

Prosperity may seem challenging to define, but it is not because when you see prosperity, you will know. Prosperity leaves clues. It is possible to predict prosperity, just like poverty. While most of the book has been on money and seed sowing for financial prosperity, it is important that we define what prosperity is. Money alone cannot be used to measure if somebody is prosperous or not.

According to the Merriam Webster Dictionary, prosperity is defined as: "the condition of being successful or thriving *especially*: economic well-being."[12]

Prosperity is discovering what you were created to do and doing it successfully. For example, a bird is prospering because it flies; the fish in the ocean and rivers are prosperous as they swim. We know an apple tree is successful when it grows, matures, and bears apples.

The purpose of the apple tree was to bear apples. If the tree fails to bear apples, it has not prospered. The issue is not the number of apples that the tree produces. While the number of apples is important,

---

[12] "Prosperity," Merriam Webster Dictionary, accessed October 30, 2020, https://www.merriam-webster.com/dictionary/prosperity

it is not the only measure that can be used to evaluate if the apple prospered or not. What is essential is that the apple tree produces fruit.

This may be a basic definition of prosperity, but it speaks volumes about how we can start evaluating if we are prospering or not.

The first thing is to identify your why. Why were you born, and what are you doing here? If you do not answer these basic yet profound and crucial questions, prosperity will elude you. There are many people who have a lot of material things, yet they are unhappy and miserable. No wonder some of these people cannot sleep because they are not satisfied.

When the focus shifts from rendering services to other people and meeting their needs to just making money, you have crossed the line. That is why the love of money becomes the root of all kinds of evil:

> For the love of money is a root of all *kinds of* evil, for which some have strayed from the faith in their greediness, and pierced themselves through with many sorrows. (1 Tim. 6:10 NKJV)

It is crucial that a significant distinction is made between prospering and the love of money from inception. Many people mix the two together. Therefore, they wrongfully equate having money to being a lover of money. While some people who have much money love money, there are also many people who have much money but do not it.

The Bible recounts two stories of people who had money, and the contrast between them is like day and night. The first person is the man Jesus Christ called the rich fool.

This man had a bountiful harvest from his fields. Then he decided to keep everything for himself.

> [The man said] "And I will say to my soul, 'Soul, you have many goods laid up for many years; take your ease; eat, drink, *and* be merry.'" But God said to him, "Fool! This night your soul will be required of you; then whose will those things be which you have provided?"
>
> [Jesus said] "So *is* he who lays up treasure for himself, and is not rich toward God." (Luke 12:19-21 NKJV)

This rich man became foolish because he forgot that it is more blessed to give than to receive. He had received an increase from God but decided that he was the source of his prosperity and would keep everything for himself. Unfortunately, his love for material things costs him everything.

Let us contrast this rich fool's actions to those of the man popularly known as the Good Samaritan. Jesus referred to this man as a certain man. But his actions have earned him the name Good Samaritan.

Nothing good was expected to come out of Samaria, but this man allowed compassion and mercy to guide his actions. As a result, his story has been told time and time again. Jesus was teaching, and a teacher of the law came to him and asked Him about inheriting eternal life. Jesus asked the teacher of the law what was written in the law, and he replied to love God and love our neighbors. Jesus said he was correct. But this man, we are told, wanted to justify himself, so he asked Jesus who his neighbor was:

> Then Jesus answered and said: "A certain *man* went down from Jerusalem to Jericho, and fell among thieves, who stripped him of his clothing, wounded *him,* and departed, leaving *him* half dead. Now by chance a certain priest came down that road. And when he saw him, he passed by on the other side. Likewise a Levite, when he arrived at the place, came and looked, and passed by on the other side. But a certain Samaritan, as he journeyed, came where he was. And when he saw him, he had compassion. So he went to *him* and bandaged his wounds, pouring on oil and wine; and he set him on his own animal, brought him to an inn, and took care of him. On the next day, when he departed, he took out two denarii, gave *them* to the innkeeper, and said to him, 'Take care of him; and whatever more you spend, when I come again, I will repay you.'

> So which of these three do you think was neighbor to him who fell among the thieves?"
>
> And he said, "He who showed mercy on him."
>
> Then Jesus said to him, "Go and do likewise." (Luke 10:30-37 NKJV)

We are not told in this story that this man was rich, but we have some clues that he was a person of means. This man was prosperous, and as the former Prime Minister Margaret Thatcher once said, "No one would remember the Good Samaritan if he'd only had good intentions; he had money as well."

This man was moved by compassion, but he also had the resources to take care of the man who had been robbed, beaten, and left to die. The Good Samaritan acted in direct contrast to the rich fool because he decided to share his wealth with somebody in need. He had compassion on behalf of another human being in need and did something about it.

Those who love money think only about themselves and will do all they can to get as much money as possible no matter upon whom they trample. They do not care about anybody else but themselves. They do not care about anybody else but themselves, and the last thing on their mind is to feel uncomfortable on behalf of another person, much less take any risk sharing and being a neighbor to the poor.

These are the people who blame the poor for their poverty and use that as an excuse not to do anything to help them out. While toxic charity is dangerous, it does not rule out the need for doing works of charity and sharing with those in need.

Take the case of the man who had fallen among thieves. He was in need of help at that moment because his life was on the line. The priest and the Levite missed this opportunity because they could not let go of their own traditions and belief system.

I am not in any way suggesting that one can second guess what prompted their inaction. But one thing is sure: the priest and the Levite lacked compassion and refused to help a person in need. Maybe they had the willingness to help but lacked the resources. Compared to the Good Samaritan, who had a pack animal and supplies with him, the priest and Levite were walking on foot. We will never know why they refused to help this man, but we know that they failed to be good neighbors. I am not saying that they loved money in any way. But the love of money causes people to be bad neighbors like the rich fool. Those who love money want to amass as much as they can and to keep as much as they can and use it for themselves.

There is another rich man, whom we looked at earlier, that came to see Jesus Christ because he was concerned about the eternal state of his soul. We are told that this young ruler was rich. In other words, he had prospered in material things. He had a great deal of money; maybe he was a millionaire or billionaire. There is no way we can know what his net worth was, but it is clear that he was rich. Yet, he recognized that he had a need. He wanted to know about the eternal state of his soul. This is what prompted him to go and look for Jesus Christ. Here is what transpired:

> Now as He was going out on the road, one came running, knelt before Him, and asked Him, "Good Teacher, what shall I do that I may inherit eternal life?"
>
> So Jesus said to him, "Why do you call Me good? No one *is* good but One, *that is,* God. You know the commandments: 'Do not commit adultery,' 'Do not murder,' 'Do not steal,' 'Do not bear false witness,' 'Do not defraud,' 'Honor your father and your mother.'"
>
> And he answered and said to Him, "Teacher, all these things I have kept from my youth."
>
> Then Jesus, looking at him, loved him, and said to him, "One thing you lack: **Go your way, sell whatever you have and give to the poor, and you will have treasure in heaven; and come, take up the cross, and follow Me."**

> But he was sad at this word, and went away sorrowful, for he had great possessions. (Mark 10:17-22 NKJV) Emphasies added.

This particular Bible verse in bold has been twisted and used by some to justify the unjustifiable. One has to look at it closely to ensure that what Jesus is saying here is understood clearly. We are not to cling to any material possessions. Our trust has to be in God and not our material possessions. Taking care of the poor is not an option; it is something that all who have been blessed by God should do and do willingly.

Jesus was not asking this man to do the impossible. God had already blessed him with resources and wanted him to use those resources to help the poor who were in need. Jesus was giving this man an opportunity to be an answer to the prayers of the poor. But the rich young ruler paid lip service to his love for God. Jesus knew it because he could read what was in his heart.

The request by Jesus to go and help the poor is reflected in the following scriptures:

> What *does it* profit, my brethren, if someone says he has faith but does not have works? Can faith save him? If a brother or sister is naked and destitute of daily food, and one of you says to them, "Depart in peace, be warmed and filled," but you do not give them

> the things which are needed for the body, what *does it* profit? Thus also faith by itself, if it does not have works, is dead. (James 2:14-17 NKJV)

Without faith, it is impossible to please God, Hebrews 11:6 tells us. But God does not need our money. People are the ones in need, and God expects us to express our love for Him by loving other people. This love is expressed through meeting their needs. Those who have been blessed must know that God is the owner of the blessings, and He expects them to let those blessings pass through them to those in need.

Here is how Jesus Christ demonstrated His love for us:

> By this we know love, because He laid down His life for us. And we also ought to lay down *our* lives for the brethren. But whoever has this world's goods, and sees his brother in need, and shuts up his heart from him, how does the love of God abide in him?
>
> **My little children, let us not love in word or in tongue, but in deed and in truth.** (1 John 3:16-18 NKJV) Emphases added.

It is cheap to say that we love God and love our neighbors. That is why we need to demonstrate this love through our actions. If you desire and pray to become prosperous and wealthy, make sure that you let the blessings flow through you. God, who has blessed you, is the owner of you and all that you have. Therefore, He can ask you to do whatever He wants and desires.

Those who love money will not listen to the voice of the Holy Spirit and will do their own thing. They will turn a blind eye to the needs around them and will spend as much as they can on their personal pleasure and entertainment.

A failure to understand that our trust should be in God and not our riches will become a stumbling block to our eternal destiny. Jesus understood this, and that prompted Him to say the following:

> Then Jesus looked around and said to His disciples, **"How hard it is for those who have riches to enter the kingdom of God!"** And the disciples were astonished at His words. But Jesus answered again and said to them, "Children, how hard it is for those who trust in riches to enter the kingdom of God! It is easier for a camel to go through the eye of a needle than for a rich man to enter the kingdom of God."
>
> And they were greatly astonished, saying among themselves, "Who then can be saved?"

> But Jesus looked at them and said, "With men *it is* impossible, but not with God; for with God all things are possible." (Mark 10:23-27 NKJV) Emphasis added.

The disciples had every reason to be astonished because many people consider those who have much money to be those who are prospering. They are seen as those who have God's blessings on them. The understanding is that these rich people must be doing something right, and if they are doing everything right, then God is happy with them.

Well, looks can be deceptive. There is more to being prosperous and pleasing God than just having money and material possessions. The laws of increase do not respect people. Those who obey them will be rewarded. This explains why a greedy and selfish individual like the rich fool had such a bountiful harvest, but he did not please God when he chose to keep everything for himself. He forgot that it was God who had given him the power to get the wealth.

This should serve as a reminder to all the so-called self-made people that God is the source of their wealth. If they want to prosper throughout eternity, they must acknowledge God and show practical love to their neighbors.

guarantee success in life? Does the book of Proverbs offer us false promises?" Here is what the lady said after asking these questions:

> My husband was a hard and loyal worker all his life, and we always had enough to eat, but we never really prospered. He was the most diligent and faithful employee in his company, but he usually got passed by for promotion, and less worthy people who just knew how to keep flattering the boss got the promotion. Just a year before he died, he actually lost his job despite 30 years of loyal service.
>
> I don't think my late husband is the only one like that. I remember a successful businessman saying,
>
> *"For every successful man who makes a lot of money, I could show you another ten who work just as hard but who just don't get the luck or the breaks!"*
>
> Does the Book of Proverbs offer us false promises?[13]

[13] Robin A. Brace, "A Question I Was Asked: 'Does Hard Work *ALWAYS* Guarantee Success in life?..***Does the Book of Proverbs Offer Us False Promises?***'" UK Apologetics,

Here is part of the response that this lady got from Robin A. Brace, the editor of the website from which this information is taken:

> I am really sorry that your husband worked hard throughout his life but never really got the breaks, and I think that many thousands of people are just like that. Yet you ate well and probably could afford good clothes and even to share a little with others at times. That would make you prosperous in a biblical sense. If you also had a relationship with Jesus Christ for many years, that is also *spiritual prosperity,* which will ultimately be far more important than material prosperity, which none of us can take with us from these brief physical lives, which we all lead. It is this spiritual prosperity in Christ which leads to *Life Eternal!*

Let us examine what this woman's complaint was. It is challenging to say a lot because we do not have all the facts. I don't know if her husband is part of the eighty-five percent of people who hate their jobs[14] but have to work because they need the money. Many

---

posted 2006, accessed October 30, 2020, ***http://www.ukapologetics.net/hardwork.html***

[14] Gallup. (2017, June 13). The world's broken workplace. Gallup.com. https://news.gallup.com/opinion/

people don't like their jobs and are not engaged. Their primary motivation is the money and not the job itself. This implies that they may think they are working hard, but their hatred of the job undermines their "hard work." It takes more than showing up to the job and clocking in and out. You must put your heart into the job and do it as unto the Lord. It is crucial that you not be an eye servant if you want to prosper.

The other thing that many have bought into is this false narrative of job security. They feel entitled to be guaranteed a job. No wonder that after thirty years of investing their lives in this company, this lady's husband was laid off. There is no such thing as job security. When you find your work and not a job, you will be secured because you can never be laid off from your work.

The other mistake many people are making is the whole idea of a job! Some have said that a job means Just Over Broke. You are paid just enough to make sure that you can survive and show up the next day for more pay. If you are paid a lot, you may not show up. No wonder many people are living paycheck to paycheck. There are many families that are just one paycheck away from losing their houses and getting into financial ruin.

---

chairman/212045/world-broken-workplace.aspx?g_source=position1&g_medium=related&g_campaign=tiles

The other mistake is that of depending on a single source of income. If you do not put some of the money you earn from your job to work for you, how will you ever be financially well off? Exchanging your time for money is the most inefficient way to prosper financially. You must learn how to produce goods and services. When you do this, you have positioned yourself for unlimited growth and increase.

It is reckless to spend your entire life building some other person's dreams. This is what you do when you are employed. This is why employment should not be something that you do your entire life.

Use the employment as a training ground for you to develop your giftedness, then deploy it to serve your generation. A job will never bring you the increase that you were created for. Show me how many employers are millionaires. You want to become an employer if you want to increase.

Please do not misunderstand me; I am not against people working. Many people get a job but never put in the time, energy, and effort to discover their giftedness, develop it, and deploy it.

All of us are born with a gift to serve our generation, and it is your responsibility to identify, develop, and deploy that gift. Don't get distracted by what other people are doing. Good is the enemy to great. A good job is not enough for you not to find what your giftedness is and deploy it. Putting your future in the hands of other people in the name of job security is a bad idea.

The response to this woman's question is worth analyzing. This is part of what Robin A. Brace wrote:

> If you also had a relationship with Jesus Christ for many years that is also *spiritual prosperity* which will ultimately be far more important than material prosperity which none of us can take with us from these brief physical lives which we all lead. It is this spiritual prosperity in Christ which leads to *Life Eternal!*

He is right. The ultimate prosperity is having a personal relationship with Jesus Christ, but this does not negate us being blessed financially or materially. God is the person who made the material things. These things are not evil. They can only become a problem when we start putting our trust in them instead of the creator. If you lie, cheat, steal, and commit any evil because you want to gain material things, that is when you have crossed the line. But if you provide goods and services and prosper, there is nothing wrong with it. Especially when you prosper and do not keep the increase and spend it on you alone. As long as you prosper and become a blessing to other people, you will prosper throughout eternity.

Here is what Jesus Christ said about what to do with our treasures:

> Do not lay up for yourselves treasures on earth, where moth and rust destroy and

> where thieves break in and steal; but lay up for yourselves treasures in heaven, where neither moth nor rust destroys and where thieves do not break in and steal. For where your treasure is, there your heart will be also. (Matt. 6:19-21 NKJV)

Jesus could not have made this statement if He did not believe that His followers were going to have treasures here on earth. This is why saying that having only spiritual prosperity is better because we cannot take material things out of this world is not presenting the complete truth. According to our Lord Jesus Christ, we can store treasures out of this world.

Seek first the kingdom of God

The first thing that you must do if you want to gain lasting prosperity is to seek first the kingdom of God: "But seek first the kingdom of God and His righteousness, and all these things shall be added to you." (Matthew 6:33 NKJV)

If you are not in God's kingdom, nothing else matters. Make sure that you have been reconciled to God and restored as a daughter or son of God. Then you can begin to seek God's kingdom by loving God and loving your neighbors as yourself. When you love, you serve. In other words, you have already been gifted to provide goods and services to other people. When you do this, all other things will be added.

Seek wisdom

While many people focus on financial prosperity, you will need more than money to do well. What you need is wisdom:

> Happy *is* the man *who* finds wisdom,
> And the man *who* gains understanding;
> For her proceeds *are* better than the profits of silver,
> And her gain than fine gold.
> She *is* more precious than rubies,
> And all the things you may desire cannot compare with her.
> Length of days *is* in her right hand,
> In her left hand riches and honor.
> Her ways *are* ways of pleasantness,
> And all her paths *are* peace.
> She *is* a tree of life to those who take hold of her,
> And happy *are all* who retain her. (Prov. 3:13-18 NKJV)

If you gain knowledge, understanding, and wisdom, you are going to do well. Wisdom is acting on the understanding that you have gained. The only way you can show that you are wise is by putting into action the knowledge that you have gathered. Many people say that they have an understanding, but their actions betray them. Can you say that you understand that a hot stove will burn your hand, yet you keep touching the hot stove? If you do, others will consider you to be foolish.

Meditate on the Word of God

Without godly counsel, you are going to go astray. The Word of God is the manual of life, and you must learn how to use it to navigate through life:

> Blessed *is* the man
> Who walks not in the counsel of the ungodly,
> Nor stands in the path of sinners,
> Nor sits in the seat of the scornful;
> But his delight *is* in the law of the Lord,
> And in His law he meditates day and night.
> He shall be like a tree
> Planted by the rivers of water,
> That brings forth its fruit in its season,
> Whose leaf also shall not wither;
> And whatever he does shall prosper. (Psalms 1:1-3 NKJV)

The symbolism of a tree planted by rivers of water used in the psalm is powerful and paints a vivid image of a life that is positioned to deliver. Water is the liquid of life, and if you have an ample supply of it, you are going to yield fruit. When you spend time in the Word of God and drink from the living water, you will never thirst again and will prosper.

The other thing that you have to do is to change those with whom you spend time. There are some people in your life who are toxic, and for you to prosper, you have to drop them. Don't listen to the counsel of people who do not walk in righteousness.

Obey the Word of God

The Word of God is the solid foundation on which you have to build. Without the Word of God, you may gain some material wealth but will lose throughout eternity. Therefore, to prosper, you have to love the law of God:

> The law of the Lord *is* perfect, converting the soul;
> The testimony of the Lord *is* sure, making wise the simple;
> The statutes of the Lord *are* right, rejoicing the heart;
> The commandment of the Lord *is* pure, enlightening the eyes;
> The fear of the Lord *is* clean, enduring forever;
> The judgments of the Lord *are* true *and* righteous altogether.
> More to be desired *are they* than gold,

> Yea, than much fine gold;
> Sweeter also than honey and the honeycomb.
> Moreover by them Your servant is warned,
> *And* in keeping them *there is* great reward.
> (Psalm 19:7-11 NKJV)

The devil likes to make some people think that God does not want us to have fun because the laws of God are too restrictive. The truth is that God does not want us to get hurt; that is why He sets boundaries for us to prosper within. All the laws of God have consequences embedded in them. When you break the laws, you suffer the consequences. No parent in their right mind will not warn their child about the dangers of touching a hot stove. The stove may be inviting and attractive to touch, but it is hot and will burn when touched. The laws of God are there to protect us and ensure that we do not get hurt. When you obey God's laws, you are going to prosper in all areas.

Trust in the Lord with all your heart

The other crucial thing you must do is to trust in the Lord with all your heart. You must have heard that you should follow your heart and do whatever comes naturally to you. Those who say this also believe that if it feels good, you should do it, and you should not deny yourself anything. This advice will enslave you and ruin your life eventually. To prosper, here is what you must do:

> Trust in the Lord with all your heart,
> And lean not on your own understanding;
> In all your ways acknowledge Him,
> And He shall direct your paths. (Prov. 3:5-6 NKJV)

The benefit of trusting in the Lord is that He is going to direct you and give you success. You will be able to walk in righteousness and integrity because you are doing what God is directing you to do. While it is good and important to believe in yourself, you must understand that believing in yourself has to be rooted in a belief in the God that made you. In other words, all credit has to be given to God because He is the source of all things and works in us both to will and act according to His good purpose (see Philippians 2:13).

Love your enemies

The call to love your enemies may appear to be counterintuitive, but it is what you must do if you want to prosper:

> But I say to you who hear: Love your enemies, do good to those who hate you, bless those who curse you, and pray for those who spitefully use you. To him who strikes you on the *one* cheek, offer the other also. And from him who takes away your cloak, do not

> withhold *your* tunic either. Give to everyone who asks of you. And from him who takes away your goods do not ask *them* back. And just as you want men to do to you, you also do to them likewise.
>
> But if you love those who love you, what credit is that to you? For even sinners love those who love them. And if you do good to those who do good to you, what credit is that to you? For even sinners do the same. And if you lend *to those* from whom you hope to receive back, what credit is that to you? For even sinners lend to sinners to receive as much back. But love your enemies, do good, and lend, hoping for nothing in return; and your reward will be great, and you will be sons of the Most High. For He is kind to the unthankful and evil. Therefore be merciful, just as your Father also is merciful. (Luke 6: 27-36 NIV)

Our natural inclination is to hate those who hate us and look for ways to punish our enemies. While this is the natural inclination of your heart, you must refuse to go down that road. It is more beneficial to learn how to love your enemies and pray for them. Don't wait for this to naturally happen because it is not going to.

You will have to be intentional about loving your enemies and those who hate you. The instruction is for you to do your part, irrespective of if your enemies have done theirs or not.

While it is natural to want the other party to move first, you must move first if you're going to prosper. Ask God to bless your enemies and wish them well in your heart. When the thoughts of hate flood your mind, fight back with a word of blessing. When your enemies prosper, it will not take anything from you. Allow God to clean up the mess for you. God Himself has promised that He will take vengeance. You are not God; allow God to do His part; meanwhile, you do your part by loving your enemies.

Planning is crucial

How many people have you met who tell you that they are walking by faith and believing God for supernatural increases and breakthroughs yet have zero plan? It has been said that a dream without goals is wishful thinking. If you have desires, goals, and ambitions without adequate planning, you will not go anywhere. The way to plenty is to do the following: "The plans of the diligent *lead* surely to plenty, But *those of* everyone *who is* hasty, surely to poverty." (Proverbs 21:5 NKJV)

Planning is going to require patience, thinking, and strategizing, without which you will fail. Just because you have discovered your giftedness does not mean that you should go out immediately and deploy your gift. Just because you have a calling, vision, or dream does not mean you should execute it immediately; you must put in the time to prepare yourself before you execute it.

Take the case of King David; after he was anointed to be king, he fled from King Saul for more than eight years. It was after this period of training that he became king. He was already an anointed king, but he had to wait for God's timing. Ample opportunities were presented along the line for him to take a shortcut to the throne, but he refused.

Another person who did not rush through their preparation was Joseph. It took thirteen years from the time he received the dream that he would be a leader over his brothers and his entire family to when he became the prime minister of Egypt. The preparatory period was equipping him with the administrative skills he would need to later become the number one administrator in Egypt.

You must have heard that it took eighty years of preparation for Moses to stand before Pharaoh and demand his people be set free. Eighty years is a long time, but that time was necessary because the task ahead of Moses was enormous. He was not only being called to free slaves but to establish a new nation made up of former slaves. This was not an easy task.

Many people are impatient and do not want to wait. They want to prosper and want it now! No wonder they fall prey to all the charlatans who masquerade in the name of God. They promise breakthroughs and massive financial returns without factoring in time.

Meet Chinese bamboo, the epitome of patience, perseverance, and preparation. Here is the story of the Chinese bamboo tree culled from the transcript of a motivational speech narrated by Les Brown:

> In the far east they have something that's called the Chinese bamboo tree. The Chinese bamboo tree takes five years to grow. They have to water and fertilize the ground where it is every day, and it doesn't break through the ground until the fifth year. But once it breaks through the ground, within five weeks it grows 90 feet tall.
>
> Now the question is does it grow 90 feet tall in five weeks, or five years?
> The answer is obvious. It grows 90 feet tall in five years.[15]

[15] "The Chinese Bamboo Tree – Les Brown Motivational Speech," Motivation Mentalist, July 23, 2018, https://motivationmentalist.com/2018/07/23/chinese-bamboo-tree-les-brown-motivational-speech/

Some accounts have it that the Chinese bamboo tree can grow up to 35 inches in a day; this is about 1.5 inches per hour.[16] Before this outward growth, the tree had been preparing for this moment for more than five years. The patience, perseverance, and preparation finally pay off big time for the tree.

You should run away as fast as you can from all who promise you fast results without any time for preparation. Don't be afraid to do your homework, plan, and wait for the right time to execute. The waiting and preparation process is not for the faint-hearted. Be ready for the naysayers to mock, ridicule, and discourage you. What you do is to keep your eyes on the prize and march forward boldly.

Don't be afraid of discomfort associated with sowing

In most farming communities, sowing is a time of hunger. The farmers have to sacrifice their precious seeds and wait for a couple of months for an increase. That is why you should not be afraid of the discomfort that is associated with sowing; you have the following promise:

[16] Anna, "Five facts about the Chinese bamboo tree," accessed November 1, 2020, https://bellechinesecalligraphy.com/five-facts-about-the-chinese-bamboo-tree/

> Those who sow in tears
> Shall reap in joy
> He who continually goes forth weeping,
> Bearing seed for sowing,
> Shall doubtless come again with rejoicing,
> Bringing his sheaves *with him.* (Psalm 126:5-6 NKJV)

After you sow, water, and wait, you will eventually harvest. If you circumvent any of these steps, you will not have a harvest. The process may not be comfortable, but the reward is going to be worth it. It may be a painful process, and you may even shed some tears, but it will not be long before you start harvesting.

Consider the case of Joseph, who was betrayed by his brothers and sold into slavery. He finally ended up in jail for walking in righteousness. But through all this ordeal, he was being prepared for greatness. It was time for him to sow some seeds that eventually brought his deliverance and lifted him to a place of prominence. It was while he was in prison that he interpreted the dream of the cupbearer, who eventually recommended his services to Pharaoh.

Your weeping will only be for a moment, and the joy of harvesting will take away the sorrow from sowing. Therefore, don't be afraid to go through any discomfort.

Be diligent

You do not only need to have a plan and strategy; you must work hard as well. There is no substitute for hard work and diligence:

> Do you see a man *who* excels in his work?
> He will stand before kings;
> He will not stand before unknown *men*.
> (Prov. 22:29 NKJV)

Prayer is critical, and you must pray. As you pray, you must also work hard because faith without works is dead. Don't fall for the promises of making money without hard work. God is not going to throw down money from heaven to you. The first command that God gave Adam was for him to work. If you want financial prosperity, be ready to work and to work hard.

Consider the seasons and read the times

You need knowledge, wisdom, and understanding to excel at making money. There is no place for laziness:

> Go to the ant, you sluggard!
> Consider her ways and be wise,
> Which, having no captain,

> Overseer or ruler,
> Provides her supplies in the summer,
> *And* gathers her food in the harvest.
> How long will you slumber, O sluggard?
> When will you rise from your sleep?
> A little sleep, a little slumber,
> A little folding of the hands to sleep—
> So shall your poverty come on you like a prowler,
> And your need like an armed man. (Prov. 6:6-11 NKJV)

There is much to learn from the ants because they are industrious and work hard. Have you ever heard the expression "as busy as an ant"? Well, ants are always busy working.

When I was a kid, ants fascinated me because they carried food particles that were many times larger than their size. Each time you see ants, they are doing something. You never see an ant idling or just standing there doing nothing. But what is even more interesting is how much the ants cooperate with each other to get their job done. If you visit Africa, you will see giant anthills that these tiny little creatures build. Yet, they do not have a leader cracking the whip on them to work hard.

Also, there is a season when you will find no ants because they have all moved underground because of weather conditions. You have to understand the time you are living in, what problems have to be solved, and the needs to be met. The opportunities to make money are in the problems that your generation is facing; identify the needs and provide solutions. When you bring solutions to the table, you will be rewarded financially.

Work hard and smart

There is no better way to end this chapter than to talk about hard work. You must till the ground. It is crucial that you put in the hard work that is necessary to gain wealth:

> He who tills his land will have plenty of bread,
> But he who follows frivolity will have poverty enough!
>
> A faithful man will abound with blessings,
> But he who hastens to be rich will not go unpunished.
>
> To show partiality *is* not good,
> Because for a piece of bread a man will transgress. (Prov. 28:19-21 NKJV)

If you want poverty to depart from you, don't waste your time on frivolity. You will remain poor if you keep sowing seeds of money yet not working hard to earn money. I have said many times throughout this book that money is a medium of exchange. The way you make money is by using your giftedness to serve other people. When you provide goods and services, people will reward you with money. This is an excellent exchange, and you should not be ashamed of it.

It is going to take more than hard work for you to succeed financially. You must work smart as well. One way to work smart is by putting some of the money you earned to work for you. That means investing your money so that it can facilitate the production of goods and services. This book is not a book about investment; there are excellent books out there, and you should check them out because investing is an excellent way to put your money to work.

If you are still wondering if your life has purpose and meaning or what your assignment is, I want you to consider the following:

> For we are His workmanship, created in Christ Jesus for good works, which God prepared beforehand that we should walk in them. (Eph. 2:10 NKJV)

There is work that God already prepared for you beforehand to do. Now is the time to discover that work and do it. God is not a slave master, and He does not expect you to work for free.

Contrary to what some hold and teach, God will reward you if you identify your work and work it hard and smart. Money is not evil and making a lot of it is not evil either. What is pure evil, and the root of all evil, is the love of money. When you love money or when it is only about the money, you will break laws and hurt other people in the process of amassing money for yourself.

If you want financial breakthrough and supernatural increase, you must identify your giftedness, develop it, and deploy it through providing goods and services to serve other people. There is no shortcut to legitimate and lasting wealth other than loving God and loving your neighbor as yourself.

When you love God, you will accept who you are because God created you in His image and likeness and declared that you are good. If you do not accept this truth after you become reconciled to God, it will be difficult to love other people. Therefore, one of the most incredible acts of worshiping God is accepting who you are in light of how God created you.

When you learn to love and accept yourself, you will love and accept other people. The love that you have for people will propel you to look for solutions for their problems and serve them with these solutions. It is in serving that you are going to get rewarded.

My story

Lastly, you may be wondering how this information applies to me personally. I am doing my best to live the message in this book. This book was written to address a problem that is plaguing the church.

About three years ago, after I got laid off the second time because of low oil and gas prices, and after much soul-searching and praying, I accepted a call to write and speak. This has not been an easy journey, but each day has made it clearer that this is what I was created to do.

My mission is to inspire, equip, and motivate other people to discover God's potential in them and take action. This is how my company, IEM APPROACH, was formed with its subsidiary IEM PRESS. Currently, I serve people in many different capacities, and it brings me great joy to finally be deploying my gifts and providing solutions.

My last words for you are to be patient and not be moved by where other people are or what they are doing. You have to identify your giftedness, develop it, and deploy it, and God will bless you as you serve other people. He is a merciful, loving, and generous God and wants to ensure that the resources you need to accomplish your mission are provided. It is not just about the money; it is about loving God and loving others.

Chapter 7

One of the Most Important Things to Consider

For what profit is it to a man if he gains the whole world, and loses his own soul? Or what will a man give in exchange for his soul? — Matthew 16:26 NKJV

Thank you so much for buying this book and reading it. Many people buy books and do not bother to read them. You are reading this chapter because you read the book. I do not know what motivated you to buy the book in the first place. But I think you would like to learn how to be successful with your money. I hope by now you understand that you need to use your giftedness to provide solutions for others to earn money. This is a noble desire that needs to be commended.

I am a student of personal growth and development, and my mission is to inspire, equip, and motivate people from all walks of life to become aware of the greater possibilities for their own lives and to take action. This has been coined into the IEM APPROACH, which is a holistic take on personal growth and development. In other words, to be truly successful, the spiritual and physical have to be in synergy. Therefore, care is taken to ensure that while we encourage people to have successful careers and pursue and achieve their goals and aspirations, care is taken to ensure that these people also do well spiritually.

This issue of the eternal state of your soul is the most important; it was placed at the end of the book because your soul is more valuable than anything else. In fact, I saved the best for last to reward you for sticking with it through the book. This is the good news that you were created for a purpose and that God loves you unconditionally.

While some do not think that the spiritual aspect of our lives is important, I am of the persuasion that the spiritual is paramount. Therefore, it is prudent to prioritize your spiritual life. While it is an excellent idea to achieve greatness in this life, it is far more profitable to achieve spiritual and eternal success. It would be a colossal failure on my part for us to have this encounter where I fail to share with you the source of my own physical and spiritual success.

This section of the book is controversial to some people, but I cannot in good conscience refuse to share with you the most important thing that has shaped and influenced my life. This is something that is well documented in my books *Coming to America: A Journey of Faith* and *Why I Refused to Become an Illegal Alien: Navigating the Complexities of the American Immigration System.*

If I refuse to share how you can get connected to the source of ALL things, I would have given you an excellent car to drive but no gasoline to put in the car. The other missing component is the key to start the car. If you are in an environment where there is zero possibility of buying fuel for the vehicle, it is useless. But not because there is anything wrong with the car; it will not serve you because it lacks the essential thing that it was manufactured to run on.

You are like that car, and for you to function to your full capacity, both now and eternally, you are going to need the power of God through the Holy Spirit working inside of you. The basic assumption I made through the book was that you have made things right with God. But this may not be the case, and I would be extremely dishonest if I did not present the following information to you.

You may be of another religious or spiritual persuasion. That is fine. The only thing I am suggesting here is that you take a close look at what I have to say because Jesus made some strong claims about how to go to God. I am referring to the God who is revealed in the Bible.

While some insist that there is one God and all roads lead to this one God, the Bible teaches that there are many different gods and different roads lead to these different gods. Therefore, there is no point insisting that all religions are trying to achieve the same thing because they are not. Superficially, they may appear to be trying to get to the same destination. But when you take a close look, you will realize that all the gods are different, and the destination is not the same.

The Bible teaches the exclusivity of Jesus Christ, especially the declaration that: "Jesus said to him, 'I am the way, the truth, and the life. No one comes to the Father except through Me.'" (John 14:6 NKJV) This is such a powerful statement with far-reaching implications that it warrants a serious investigation. I know you are somebody who wants to win. You desire to be at the top of your game. I trust you to do the right thing by investigating this claim made by Jesus Christ. This chapter does not have all the information, but there are tons of resources out there that can help.

There is nothing more important than being connected to God. While many may argue that there is one God and many different roads to this God, I will object to that conclusion. All the religions in the world have different gods, and there is no need for all the gods to be the same.

Some are incredibly uncomfortable holding any discussion that involves God because they do not want to offend people. The problem with such a worldview is that such people are treating something that is extremely important casually. We all know that if we have a diagnosis of brain cancer, we will not want just any doctor to operate on our brain. Anybody who is wise will look for the best of the best to conduct the surgery.

You will meticulously gather knowledge about the different specialists available and gain some understanding of what separates them. Then you will make an informed and wise decision of selecting the best to operate on your brain. You do not hold a vote and decide what doctor to operate on your brain based on popular support or which doctor is trending. You would not care less about the doctor's popularity as long as they are competent and have the necessary skills and expertise to take care of you.

Then why is it that when it comes to spiritual matters, people seem not to be as diligent as they are supposed to be? Is it because they do not know what is at stake? May I suggest that your soul is more important than your physical body? In fact, there is no price tag for your soul. Let me put it this way: all the wealth in the world is not enough to buy your soul. Therefore, you have to pay close attention to the eternal destiny of your soul.

I am not trying to force you to embrace some particular religious tradition because I am not a religious person. What I am suggesting here is that you carefully consider the claims that Jesus Christ made and what He has accomplished for you already. My sincere hope is that you will put in the time and effort necessary to acquire the right knowledge and gain the understanding that you need to make a wise decision regarding the eternal destiny of your soul.

There is nothing more important than your soul. And you do not need the approval of others to make things right with God. On the contrary, making things right with God is an individual decision, and it is not popular. Consider the following statement that Jesus Christ made:

> Enter by the narrow gate; for wide *is* the gate and broad *is* the way that leads to destruction, and there are many who go in by it. Because narrow *is* the gate and difficult *is* the way which leads to life, and there are few who find it. (Matt. 7:13-14 NKJV)

According to this verse, there are too many people who are walking on the road to destruction. This implies that if you go by what is popular, you will be following the crowd and will end up in destruction. There is no need for you to follow the crowd. Get on the narrow path that few are walking on, and you will find life. This is not just any type of life. It is eternal life that Jesus Christ Himself gives. Here is your opportunity to get on the path of eternal life. Do not allow what is popular and trending to rob you of eternal life.

Having an eternal perspective is the ultimate because, at the end of the day, it is the eternal that matters. People have looked for the fountain of youth over the ages, and there is a lot of research right now to understand aging and how to reverse it. Even if we were to find the fountain of youth and drink from it so that we remain young forever, life on earth would still have many changes for us. This also implies that even if we reverse aging and make sure that we remain young here on earth, we would still face many other challenges because we are living in a fallen world with many different problems.

I say all this to emphasize the importance of looking forward to our true and final home, where we will be with our Heavenly Father forever and ever. While life on earth is great, life in heaven is going to be greater and more fulfilling. This is something that all of God's children have to look forward to.

But if you are not yet a child of God, here is your opportunity to learn how to become a child of God. You cannot afford to neglect this crucial issue or put it off for another day. Let this be a sign that it is time for you to make things right with God.

Available for speaking engagements:

If you want to invite Dr. Tangumonkem to come and speak, you can call him using this number 214-908-3963 or email him at eternalkingdom101@gmail.com

Here are his social media handles:

https://www.erictangumonkem.com

https://www.linkedin.com/in/drtangumonkem/

https://twitter.com/DrTangumonkem

https://www.facebook.com/drtangumonkem

tangumonkem.tumblr.com

https://instagram.com/tangumonkem/

http://www.pinterest.com/erictangumonkem/

https://vimeo.com/user23079930

https://www.youtube.com/c/EricTangumonkem

Other Resources by the Author

Coming to America: A Journey of Faith

Do you struggle with trusting God with your finances? Feel that God is calling you to do something big but you can't see how it will be accomplished? Fear that He has abandoned you after starting your journey of faith? Coming to America: A Journey of Faith is Eric Tangumonkem's story of wrestling with these thoughts and doubts. God called him to America from Cameroon to pursue graduate studies at the University of Texas at Dallas, but he had no money to put towards this dream. In this book, Tangumonkem shares his journey of learning to trust God as he stepped out in faith and came to America despite a lack of funds. He also shares some of his formative experiences prior to this call-experiences that will encourage readers in their faith. Tangumonkem's life is a testimony to the faithfulness of God, and he is careful to give Him all of the glory.

Order: https://www.iemapproach.com/shop

The Use and Abuse of Titles in The Church

This book examines reasons behind the disturbing proliferation of titles in Christendom in recent times by seven distinguished Christian professionals. The book challenges readers to stay on the straight and narrow road, which celebrates ministers with titles bestowed based on sound Biblical foundations, while shunning those with titles associated with self-promotion and doctrinal errors. The book also provides the following actionable insights:· How to identify the proper use of titles · A history on the use of titles in Christendom How to avoid the pitfalls of acquiring bogus titles An understanding of the relationship between titles and leadership.

Order: https://www.iemapproach.com/shop

Seven Success Keys Learned From My Father

This is a book about my father, my teacher, my role model and hero. A man of passion like any other man, but a man of exceptional qualities and abilities as well. The following are the seven keys to success my father passed to me: Fear of God, Humility, Education, Integrity, Hard work, Prayer and Vision. All these keys have been instrumental in making me who I am today. In addition to these keys, my father was present when we were growing up. He made it a point of duty to talk the talk and walk the walk before us. This book illustrates how these seven keys to success were interwoven in our day-to-day lives and how they have opened unprecedented doors of success to me. My sincere prayer for you as you read this book is that these keys will open all doors for you and bring the success you desire so strongly. Amen!

Order: https://www.iemapproach.com/shop

Viajando a América: Un Camino de Fe (Spanish Edition)

¿Lucha con confiar en Dios con sus finanzas? Siente que Dios le está llamando a hacer algo grande, pero usted no puede ver la forma en que se llevará a cabo? ¿Teme a que Él le ha abandonado después de comenzar su camino de fe?

Viajando a América: Un Camino de Fe es la historia de Eric Tangumonkem, de su lucha con estos pensamientos y dudas. Dios lo llamó a América desde Camerún para realizar estudios de posgrado en la Universidad de Texas en Dallas, pero no tenía dinero para seguir este llamado. En este libro, Tangumonkem comparte su viaje de aprender a confiar en Dios cuando caminó en la fe y llegó a Estados Unidos a pesar de su falta de fondos. También comparte algunas de sus experiencias formativas previas a esta convocatoria-experiencias que estimularán a los lectores en su fe. La vida de Tangumonkem es un testimonio de la fidelidad de Dios, y él tiene cuidado en darle toda la.

Order: https://www.iemapproach.com/shop

MON ODYSSÉS AMÉRICAINE: UNE EXPÉRIENCE DE FOI (French Edition)

As-tu du mal à confier tes soucis financiers au Seigneur? Ressens-tu que Dieu t'appelle à faire quelque chose de grand, mais tu ne sais comment cela va se réaliser? Crains-tu qu'il va t'abandonner en chemin? Mon Odyssée Américaine: une expérience de foi est l'histoire d'Éric Tangumonkem et de sa lutte contre le doute et les pensées susmentionnées. Dieu l'a appelé depuis le Cameroun pour aller poursuivre ses études supérieures à l'Université du Texas à Dallas, mais il n'avait pas d'argent pour réaliser ce rêve. Dans ce livre, le Dr Tangumonkem partage avec vous les péripéties de son voyage qui l'ont amené à faire davantage confiance à Dieu alors qu'il se rendit aux États-Unis par la foi. Il partage également certaines des expériences qui l'ont bâti avant même son appel – expériences qui vont encourager les lecteurs dans leur foi. La vie du Dr Tangumonkem est un témoignage de la fidélité de Dieu à qui il rend toute la gloire.

Order: https://www.iemapproach.com/shop

God's Supernatural Agenda: 7 Secrets to Lasting Wealth and Prosperity

Is there something more valuable than money, precious stones, silver, and gold? Do you desire to be wealthy and prosperous? Are you already wealthy and prosperous, yet you feel empty and unsatisfied? Are you uncomfortable talking about money because it is "the root of all evil"? This book will not present shortcuts or get-rich-quick schemes, but important principles, laws, and processes involved in generating lasting wealth.

You see, God desires for ALL of us to prosper today and for all eternity. He has a divine reason for that desire, and He has given us the way to attain it. God's Supernatural Agenda: 7 Secrets to Lasting Wealth and Prosperity presents His blueprint for prosperity and explains why it is what truly matters.

Order: https://www.iemapproach.com/shop

Racism, Where Is Your Sting?
A provocative look at the beginning and the end of racism

Each time the issue of racism is mentioned, tensions immediately run high, reason is thrown out the window, and emotional outbursts run rampant. Even though a lot of effort has been done to fight it, the devastating consequences continue to this day.

In this book, Dr. Tangumonkem challenges the status quo and presents a perspective that is both provocative and inspirational. Contrary to what you hear from those stoking the flames of racism and fermenting hate and bigotry, we are not at the mercy of racism. In fact, he dives deep into history to explain why the tendency to be racist is present in each one of us, regardless of skin color. The good news is that the victory has already been won — all we need is to live it out. When we stare right at this supercharged issue with fresh, unfiltered eyes, a seismic shift happens. Perhaps, the light at the end of racism is in sight.

Order: https://www.iemapproach.com/shop

The Intersection of Faith, Migration and God's Mission: A call for the people of God in the West to engage in Mission Dei

"Our missionary brothers, sisters, sons, daughters, husbands, and wives would travel thousands of miles to share the gospel to people in faraway lands. They are willing to sacrifice all to share the love of God with these people. Times are changing. Now, God is bringing people from foreign lands right to our shores. Is this a new mission? What is His reason? Unfortunately, the present political climate and rhetoric are making it extremely difficult, if not impossible, for us to have a level-headed discussion when it comes to this topic of migration. It seems the people of God are divided on what to do as well. We have been tasked to be the light of the world. We cannot hide behind nationalistic tendencies or political correctness. We must stand up and be the light in a time of darkness. We must speak the truth in love in a time of fear. We must advocate for peace in a time of hatred."

Order: https://www.iemapproach.com/shop

From Cameroonian to American Citizen: A Journey of Faith by ERIC TANGUMONKEM

When it comes to the problem of illegal immigration, divisive rhetoric has shut out the voice of reason and common sense. Polarization has resulted in two extreme views--either open the borders wide and allow the free movement of people and goods, or close the borders and prevent people from coming in. The solution is somewhere in the middle . . . if we are willing to listen to one another. From Cameroonian to American Citizen: A Journey of Faith, chronicles the long and arduous journey of one man who immigrated legally and believes that the cost of allowing America's present immigration crisis to remain unresolved is too high. Drawing upon his deep Judeo-Christian roots, this newly-naturalized US citizen sets forth Bible-based solutions that emphasize the need to be our brother's keeper—to show love, mercy, and compassion and at the same time be fair and just.

Order: https://www.iemapproach.com/shop

For Every Excuse, There is a Solution: 7 Reasons Why You Should Stop Giving Excuses and Start Providing Solutions

While it is a natural thing to give excuses, this book will be arguing that giving excuses is not good enough. The reason is, that each time excuses come up it is an indication of the possibility to provide solutions. While these opportunities may be hidden in pain, injustices, discrimination, and hatred, it takes seeing beyond excuses to come up with solutions. The way to become significant and make an impact is by providing solutions. But you will never rise to the occasion if all you do is give excuses. You will remain stuck where you are if you keep giving "good excuses." The bitter truth is that no matter how good you think your excuses are, the only thing they are doing for you is keeping you stuck in your present predicament.

Order: https://www.iemapproach.com/shop

The Priesthood of Every Believer: A Call to Step into Your True Vocation

"Do you often wonder what your true vocation is?Are you struggling to serve God, do your job or run your business?Do you think serving God full time is only for a select, anointed, and dedicated few?These and many other questions have been answered in this book. Contrary to what many believe today, the clergy-laity divide is a human invention with no biblical backing. The consequences of operating under this divide are far-reaching, and now is the time to do something about it. There is one priesthood, and it is the priesthood of every believer. The notion of a priesthood within a priesthood is not what God intended. This explains why the body of Christ is not as healthy and vibrant as it is supposed to be. We have not been called into a religion or to just the observation of ordinances, but to have a relationship with God and to function as His priests."

Order: https://www.iemapproach.com/shop

Where is Your Home?: A Call for Christian Immigrants to Engage in Mission Dei

You might have migrated from your country of birth for the sole purpose of securing better education or greener pastures. However, God has a bigger plan for your life, and He wants to use you to be light and salt in a world that is decaying and walking in darkness. It is a privilege to be called by God to partner with Him to accomplish this important mission. That is not to say that securing a good education or greener pastures is negative. But these things are secondary to the responsibility of being a priest of God, and you should never disobey God for any economic or worldly gain. This sums up our love for God. When you love God, you will love people. And when you love people, you will share with them the greatest ever news. This is your opportunity to participate in Mission Dei.

Enhance your Marriage: The surprising benefits of exercising as husband and wife

Marriage is like a three-legged stool! Every successful marriage has three legs that it stands on, and it is impossible to build a strong and enduring marriage without communication, money, and sex. Most marriage experts have identified three aspects of marriage that MUST be present and functioning well for any successful marriage. All three aspects feed into each other, and the more you strengthen one, the stronger the other two become, and the deeper the level of commitment and the more enjoyable the marriage will be. We have added a catalyst that will enhance communication, money, and sex in every marriage. In fact, exercise is more than a catalyst; it is the bedrock on which the three legs stand. This book will enhance, energize and synergize revolutionize your marriage beyond your greatest imagination.

Order: https://www.iemapproach.com/shop

A 90 Day Challenge for Husbands and Wives to Exercise Together: A Step by Step Guide on How to Get This Done

Have you tried unsuccessfully to exercise with your husband or wife? Do you dread the thought of exercising together because you argue and fight? You are not alone! Many married couples find it difficult to exercise because they do not have a road map. Fear and worry no more; we are putting an end to this. That is why we have put this resource to help you learn how to use one stone and shoot two birds. In other words, you will be maximizing your time by exercising together for the sake of your health and your marriage. The 30 to 45 minutes that you will spend together exercising as husband and wife will have a multiplier effect on your health, quality of sex, communication, increase your intimacy and save you tons of money. You cannot go wrong exercising together as a couple. This roadmap results from close to a decade of exercising together and regularly as husband and wife. All we ask of you is to invest the next ninety days and see your marriage energize, revitalized, and synergized.

Order: https://www.iemapproach.com/shop

Nothing is Free: Can it Be You are Poor Because You Like Free Stuff?

Nothing is free! There is always a cost. If you get it free, it is because somebody paid for it. Next time you are about to accept a free offer or service, think about the person bearing the cost. Free will only last as long as the person paying can afford it. The person must be able and willing to continue giving the free stuff. If any of these components is missing, the chain will be broken, and the free stuff will stop flowing. This is why charity, in the long run, is toxic and unsustainable.

Free in the long run is not sustainable because the process of productivity is short-circuited. For productivity to continue unabated, it is imperative that giving and receiving are not interrupted. The giver must accept, and the receiver must provide. If this give and receive cycle is broken because it has become a one-way street, productivity will suffer.

It is counter-intuitive to think that being just at the receiving end will hurt the receiver eventually. If you believe that receiving free stuff from other people is smart, you sacrifice your productivity and remain poor. As harsh as this may sound, there is a connection between the desire for free stuff and poverty.

Order: https://www.iemapproach.com/shop

Made in United States
Orlando, FL
05 November 2026

90230221R00121